The Folklore of The British Isles
General Editor: Venetia J. Newall

The Folklore of Ireland

Diarmaid and Gráinne

The Folklore of Ireland

Sean O'Sullivan

Drawings by John Skelton

B. T. BATSFORD LTD LONDON

First published 1974

© Sean O'Sullivan 1974

ISBN 0 7134 2803 1

Printed in Great Britain by
Bristol Typesetting Co. Ltd. Bristol
for the Publishers
B. T. Batsford Ltd 4 Fitzhardinge Street London W1H 0AH

Foreword

I first met Sean O'Sullivan (O Súilleabháin) in September 1969 at *The Anglo-American Folklore Conference*, held at the Ditchley Foundation near Oxford, when our Celtic colleagues from the neighbouring countries of these islands were present, together with the participants from America and England. In all these lands folklore studies were far in advance of England, and one object of the Conference was to set a new course for our own endeavours. That advance is now under way, but I still read with envy the paper which Sean O'Sullivan presented at Ditchley: *Research Opportunities in the Irish Folklore Commission*.

The Irish Folklore Commission is now 39 years old and, as the Department of Folklore in University College, Dublin, has in its possession, as Professor Dorson puts it: 'The sources for a thousand books.' When the Commission was set up in 1935 it was noted that, for instance, the parish of Carna in West Galway had more unrecorded folktales than the whole of Europe. This indicates the unique wealth of data to be drawn on, and explains the make-up of the present volume. The fact that it varies slightly from its predecessors arises from the importance of making this wonderful material available to a wider public.

Sean O'Sullivan has been Archivist of the Irish Folklore Commission since its foundation. In 1963 he brought out with Reidar Christiansen an Index to the 43,000 versions of popular tales collected during the Commission's first twenty-one years. *(The Types of the Irish Folktale)*, and his knowledge of all this material is boundless. Of the value of these treasures from the past, he himself has said: 'Some survivals lead us back to the habits of hundreds and even thousands of years ago; all are worthy of sympathetic approach for the light they may throw on the mental processes of our ancestors.'

Ireland has been lucky both in the diligence and the deep understanding shown by her folklore researchers. Sean O'Sullivan upholds the splendid tradition shared with his colleagues, which goes back through innumerable eminent personalities – Douglas Hyde, the first Irish President and a notable folklorist, W. B. Yeats, Lady Gregory, and many others too numerous to mention. Even the Anglo-Irishman, Croker, who originally did field-work in Ireland, was noted for the sympathetic relations he established with his subjects.

Croker's first book, *Researches in the South of Ireland*, appeared exactly 150 years ago. Described by Professor Dorson in his chapter on 'The Antiquary Folklorists', Croker drew on the tradition established by Hone and Aubrey, to present material which inspired the Grimms and Sir Walter Scott, and broadened the horizons of folklore.

Aubrey's view, almost three centuries ago, was that: 'Old Customs and old wives fables are grosse things but . . . 'tis a pleasure to consider the Errours that enveloped former ages, as also at present.' This is the antiquarian outlook *par excellence*. To appreciate the immense strides made in folklore studies, it is not only necessary to consider the advances in technique and scope of collection: still more important is the standpoint from which the material is viewed. No one has explained this better than Sean O'Sullivan: 'In a sense, folk belief is a correlative of the science of higher cultures. It tries in its own way to find answers to many questions about life and the world in general. Although it does this wrongly, it has, however, a certain kind of logicality.'

London University
April 1974   Venetia Newall

Contents

Foreword		5
Maps		8-9
Acknowledgment and Dedication		10
Introduction		11
I	MYTHOLOGICAL AND HERO TALES	17

1 Balor and Gaibhde the Smith 17—2 The Fate of the Sons of Uisneach 23—3 Diarmaid and Gráinne 30—4 Finn and the Big Man 35—5 Youth, the World and Death 43—6 The Everlasting Fight 46—7 Cú, the Smith's Son 53

II	ORDINARY FOLKTALES	67

8 Judas 67—9 The Best Way to God 70—10 The King of Sunday 74—11 The Dry and Wet Funeral Days 79—12 The Twining Branches 83

III	LEGENDS AND FOLK BELIEF—	86

13 Fated to be Hanged 87—14 The Mouthless Child 90—15 Saint Colmcille and Tory Island 91—16 Sean Slammon's Dream 94—17 The Fairy Frog 100—18 The Cakes of Oatmeal and Blood 105—19 The Spirit, the Sailor and the Devil 109—20 Seoirse de Barra and the Water-horse 113—21 The Conneelys and the Seals 116—22 The Wounded Seal 120—23 The Fork Against the Wave 123—24 The Soul as a Butterfly 126

IV	HISTORICAL TRADITION	129

25 The 'Danes' 129—26 Cromwell and O'Donnell 132

V	FOLK PRAYERS	137
VI	POPULAR CHARMS	141
VII	PROVERBS (THREES AND FOURS)	147
VIII	RIDDLES	153
IX	SONGS AND BALLADS	155

27 The Maid of Magheracloone 156—28 Down by Mount Callan's Side 157—29 The Foot of Rooska Hill 159—30 Famous Kildorrery Town 160—31 The Alfred de Snow 162—32 Francie Hynes 163

Notes	167
Select Bibliography	179
Index of Tale Types	183
Motif Index	184
General Index	187

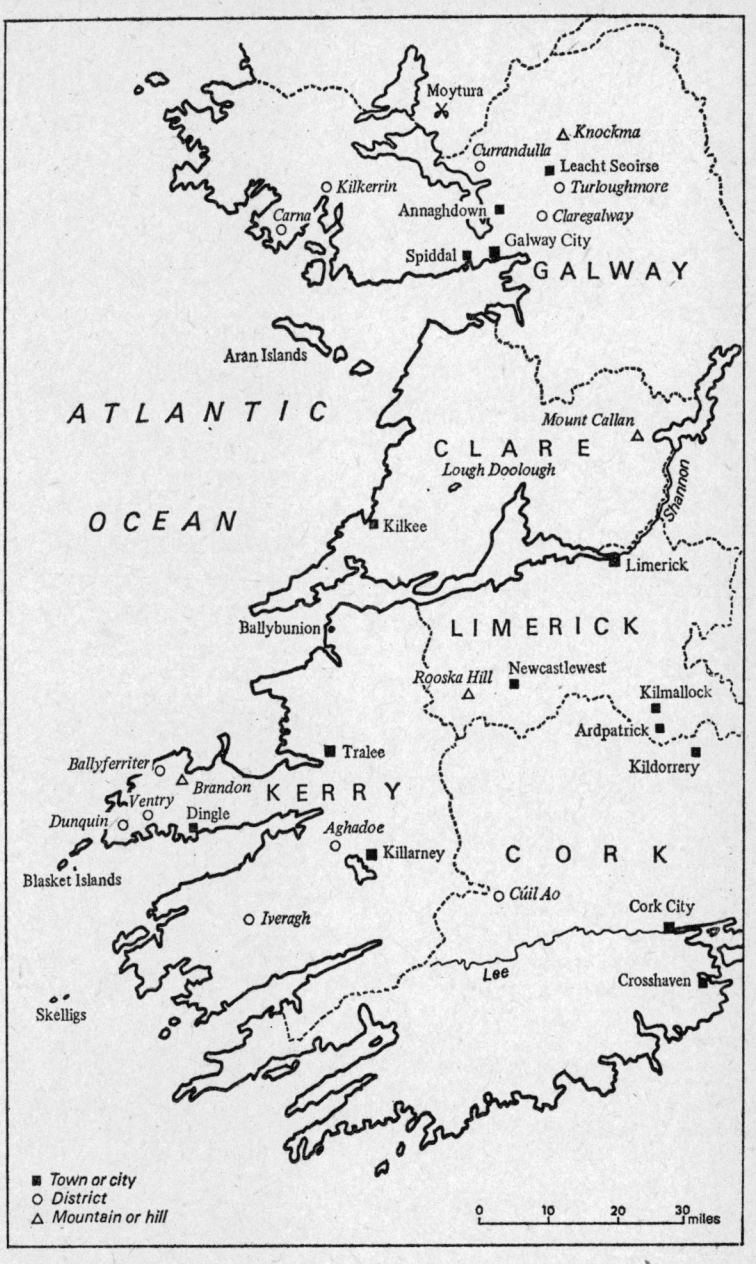

ACKNOWLEDGMENT AND DEDICATION

I wish to thank Professor Bo Almqvist, Director of the Department of Irish Folklore, University College, Dublin 4, for allowing me to use the folklore manuscripts.

To him I dedicate this volume.

Introduction

IRELAND HAS THE OLDEST vernacular literature in Western Europe. When Christianity was introduced to that country in the fifth century it brought with it a knowledge of the art of writing, and the monks used Latin as a vehicle for their writings for a couple of centuries. From the eighth century onwards, however, examples of the Old Irish language were committed to writing in the form of glosses (explanatory notes to Latin texts). The oldest surviving Irish manuscripts preserving literary and scholarly material were written in the twelfth century, and much ancient lore survives only in manuscripts from the fourteenth and fifteenth centuries.

The Irish monks and later scribes turned from Latin to the Irish language of their time when committing to writing the lore which had until then been preserved and transmitted orally. Dr Robin Flower, commenting on the large body of legendary lore which sought to explain the origins of names of individuals and places, has said that 'by the accretion of centuries there came into existence a large body of literature in prose and verse, forming a kind of Dictionary of National Topography, which fitted the famous sites of the country each with its appropriate legend. It was one of the obligations of the poet to have this knowledge ready at call . . .' This type of lore, together with much mythological and genealogical material, is to be found in the large corpus of Irish literary material which has been preserved in old manuscript collections, along with tales of various kinds.

Looking at Ireland from the traditional folklore angle in our own day, three things must be borne in mind. Firstly, Ireland's geographical position as an island on the extreme western edge of Europe ensured that, while its people were close enough to borrow lore and ideas from their European neighbours, they were enabled at the same time to preserve a fairly accurate picture of what belonged to themselves traditionally. By analogy with a pool of water into which a stone is cast, it can be seen that much of what had originally been found in continental Europe survived later only on the ultimate shores of the great land-mass and its islands. Secondly, Ireland, for good or ill, escaped physical occupation by the Romans. And thirdly, it has been able, through the interest and labours of individuals in the nineteenth century and Government action over almost the past forty years, to preserve from oblivion a substantial portion of the still living oral traditions of its people.

In 1935 the Irish Government in Dublin established the Irish Folklore Commission for the purpose of collecting and preserving for posterity as much as possible of what remained of Ireland's traditional lore. Since that time, a team of full-time collectors, varying in strength from ten in 1942 to the present (1973) five, has worked in various parts of Ireland, with strong concentration on the Irish-speaking areas along the south and west coasts where the Gaelic tradition was still rich. Ediphone machines were used for the recording of sustained narrative, such as folktales, local history and songs, as well as music. Side by side with these full-time collectors, some sixty part-time workers were also employed as collectors during their holidays or in whatever spare time they could devote to the work.

By 1937 it had become evident that, on account of the richness of the material to be recorded, additional collection on a much wider scale would have to be undertaken. The senior children in the 5,000 primary schools which were administered by the Department of Education of the Dublin Government were allowed by the Department to spend their normal composition time (in Irish and

English) in writing down in school various types of traditional lore which they had, under their teachers' guidance, collected previously from their parents and elderly neighbours. This Schools' Scheme lasted for a year and a half and secured for the Commission about a half-million pages of manuscript folklore from the Twenty-six Counties.

When it became evident as a result of the Schools' Scheme that many of the teachers had a deep presonal interest in the traditional lore of their districts, it was decided to ask for their further co-operation by replying to questionnaires on particular subjects. Six hundred of them answered one hundred queries of that kind during the succeeding years, thus making possible a coverage, both wide and deep, of many facets of Irish lore.

As a result of the collecting activities which I have mentioned, the Department of Folklore, which is now part of University College in Dublin, has in its possession one and a half million pages of written folklore, together with thousands of disc-and tape-recordings, and a very large photographic collection illustrative of Irish life. To back this up, for the purpose of comparative study, the Department has a fine library of folklore books and journals from Ireland and foreign countries.

Indexes have already been made up-to-date of the names of all collectors of various kinds, as well as of over 40,000 people whose lore has been recorded. Similarly, the districts from which folklore has been obtained are listed on cards, referring to the pages of the bound manuscript volumes on which their lore is to be found. An index of the subject-matter is also in process of being made.

In selecting the tales for this volume, I have tried to give examples which would be of interest to readers who may have no knowledge of Irish traditional storytelling. The selected tales, like most of these in our folklore collection, were recorded in the Irish language, and in translating them, I have endeavoured as far as possible to give some of the flavour of the originals. It must be remembered, however, that all folktales live only on the lips of their narrators; when heard even on a tape or disc, or when read in a manuscript or on the printed page, only a lifeless echo of the original is heard; and this lack is further accentuated when translation into a second language has been carried out.

A few words about the nature of the oral folktale may not be out of place here, as the contents of the present volume consist mainly of examples of it. Scholars are now in general agreement that each tale which has a rather involved plot was originally composed by one person in one place at one time. The only exception to this might be some very short animal tales, consisting of a single episode or two, which, it is conceded, could possibly have arisen independently in more than one country. An involved tale might, on occasion, have been committed to writing before it entered the oral stream, but, like all tales, would draw heavily on motifs in oral currency. It is probable, however, that most ordinary folktales began their life as oral compositions. All are anonymous. If one of them was a good, interesting story, it first circulated locally and, if it fitted into the traditional mould of storytelling, it spread over a larger area as it continued to be told.

Each oral tale was enabled to keep its original, integral form by being heard and retold by good narrators and by the reaction and comments of critical audiences who might have already heard it on other occasions. That a folktale can retain its identity while adapting itself to suit local conditions in each new area where it came to be told is well-known. Take the oral tale, known in English as 'Cinderella', for example. Two studies of this tale have been made at different times by Miss M. R. Cox of England (1893) and Mrs Anna Birgitta Rooth of Sweden (1951). They used some 700 versions of the tale, which had been collected from oral tradition in many countries of the world. The basic tale remained the same wherever it was told and changed only in minor details to suit new cultures and civilisations. The ability of oral tales to pass, for the most part unchanged, over linguistic, geographical and cultural boundaries through the centuries of their life makes them one of the outstanding phenomena of popular art.

The oldest folktale known is that of 'The Two Brothers', a version of which has been discovered on an Egyptian papyrus, written about 1500 BC. It may have had a long oral history even before that date. Versions of it have been found in a great many countries, and it has been recorded almost 400 times in Ireland during the past forty years. Again, Herodotus described in the fifth century how he had heard an oral version of the 'Rhampsinitus' (Thief) story in Egypt. He commented that he did not believe the story to be true; it was a good tale, however, and has been found as an oral tale in scores of countries since his time.

The oral tales found in any single country may be segregated into two main categories: those which originated in that country (national tales) and those borrowed from outside (international tales). Both types are represented in this volume. Thousands of tales of the latter kind have been listed in the Aarne-Thompson register, *The Types of the Folk-tale,* and almost a thousand of them have been told in Ireland by the winter fireside, at wakes, in fishing-boats and on other suitable occasions. The national cycles of tales in Ireland and in the Gaelic-speaking areas of Scotland included mythological tales, those about the Red Branch Knights of Ulster, the Fianna and many other hero-tales. Some examples of Irish versions are given in this volume, along with others which do not belong to either category. The national tales of various kinds are generally distinguished by their heroic atmosphere and, in many cases, by the florid, descriptive language which includes 'runs' (rhetorical descriptions of challenges, journeys, voyages, combats and similar events).

Until the introduction of reading matter in print, the Irish people, like all others, had to rely on their own resources for entertainment. This consisted mainly of conversation, storytelling, singing, dancing and music, games and sports, as well as social occasions. Storytelling has been described as 'one of the oldest one-man shows on earth'. Its place has now been taken, however, by books and other printed matter, as well as by radio and television. In Ireland, tales which had previously been told in the Irish language passed over into English only to a very small extent. The oral tale is now a thing of the past in Western Europe. Only in Ireland (in the Irish-speaking areas) and in the Gaelic-speaking parts of Scotland can narrators of traditional tales still be found. Even in those two areas, however, audiences are now almost completely lacking. Without an appreciative audience, the traditional storyteller has no longer a function, so we find ourselves at the end of an era.

None of the versions of tales and legends which I have translated for inclusion in this volume has ever been published, in either Irish or English, until now.

The ballads are given in their original versions in English. The proverbial triads, the riddles, folk prayers and charms, in translation, are a few samples of the popular oral art of the Irish-speaking world.

Folk belief, which forms a very important part of oral tradition in Ireland, will be illustrated to a certain extent in the legends which follow the main folktales.

I Mythological and Hero Tales

1 Balor and Gaibhde the Smith

IRISH MYTHOLOGY, VAGUE IN DETAIL and varied in scope though it may be, gives an insight into the ancient pagan world, which cannot be found elsewhere. Greek and Roman influences seem to be absent. It abounds in fantasy, magic and primitive wonder. The two chief tales of this cycle are known as *The Wooing of Étain* and *The Battle of Moytura*. According to Irish mythology, Lugh, the most colourful figure among the divine Tuatha Dé Danann, killed with a sling-shot his greatest opponent, 'Balor of the Evil Eye', at the Second Battle of Moytura. According to tradition, it required four men to raise the lid of Balor's baleful eye; when uncovered, it could disable an army with its poisonous gaze. The god, Balor, one-eyed like Polyphemus, figures in the following story. He lived on Tory Island off the coast of Donegal and, according to a prophesy, could be killed only by his own grandson. The story tells how, despite Balor's careful guard over his daughter, his grandson came into the world and encompassed Balor's death. Fused into the tale is an account of Balor's attempt to gain possession of the wonderful milk-bearing cow, An Ghlas Ghaibhleann, owned by Gaibhde the Smith, who lived on the mainland. This cow figures in many other legends in Ireland also.

The Tuatha Dé Danann were a group of invaders of Ireland, according to Irish mythology. They were said to have acquired magical powers during their sojourn in the northern islands of the world. They defeated the Fir Bholg, who had reached Ireland earlier, but were in turn defeated by the Sons of Míl (Milesians).

The *geasa* mentioned early in the tale were a form of magical injunction imposed either by someone on himself or by another character as a demand that a certain order be carried out.

Gaibhde the Smith and his mother were living in Magheraroarty, in County Donegal. They were miserably poor and hadn't either a cow or a calf. One night a grey cow came to their door. There had been a fair at the cross-roads that day, and they thought that the cow might have strayed from there. Gaibhde's mother said it would be better to put the cow into the byre in order that she could milk her, and they would keep her until somebody claimed her. When the cow was milked, she would fill the vessel, no matter whether it was large or small, but would not give another tint of milk beyond that.

Gaihbde went to Mass the following Sunday and told the congregation that a cow had come to his house the night of the fair, and that the owner could have her back, if he came for her. Nobody came to claim the cow during the next week. Gaibhde made the same announcement at another church the following Sunday, but still nobody came for the cow.

Balor was living in Tory island at that time and he heard about the wonderful cow, so he went to the mainland to see if he could get her to buy. But Gaibhde the Smith wouldn't sell her at all. So one night Balor took a boat and double crew to the mainland; they took the cow out of the byre and dragged her, tail foremost, down the strand to the boat. When Gaibhde the Smith got up next morning, the cow was missing. He found the track of her feet on the strand, as if she had come up along it from the sea, but no track led downwards. He went up and down the strand all day, trying to make out where she had gone to. At last he caught sight of a small stone coracle, in which a boy was sitting. He went down to the high-water mark and spoke to the boy.

'You are looking for the Glas Gaibhleann, the best cow that ever came to a house,' said the boy. 'Balor has taken her to Tory.'

He invited Gaibhde the Smith to sit into the coracle, saying that he would take him to Tory. Gaibhde did so, and they set out for the island.

There was a prophecy that Balor would never die until he was killed by his own grandson. So Balor put all his children to death as soon as they were born, except one daughter. He confined her, with twelve waiting-maids, in a castle, and spread flour on the ground for a quarter-mile at each side of the castle, so that any man who tried to reach it would leave his foot-prints on it. The daughter had grown to be a young woman at this time.

When Gaibhde the Smith and the boy reached Tory, the boy took Gaibhde on his back and took him over the flour without leaving a trace. The boy was from the otherworld and he would leave no marks anywhere he went. The two of them went into the castle where the women were, and there was great rejoicing—the women were as glad as if the men had fallen down from Heaven! They stayed there until next morning; Gaibhde the Smith was with Balor's daughter, and the boy of the coracle was with the twelve waiting-women. Gaibhde wanted to find out from Balor's daughter how he could recover the cow; she said that she didn't know, but she would do all she could to help him. When they got up next morning, the boy asked Gaibhde the Smith to go to Balor and ask him for the cow, and told him that he would help him to perform any task that Balor would impose.

Balor said that he would give him the cow if he consumed nine cow-hides, horns, tails and all: Gaibhde said that he would try. The cow-hides were placed in front of him. Gaibhde took the edge of one of them in his teeth, as if he were going to eat it, and the boy, who was invisible to Balor, swept the hides out of sight, as if

Gaibhde had eaten them. Balor then ordered Gaibhde to drink the mill-race dry. Gaibhde said that he would, and no sooner had he laid his lips to the water than the boy had caused it all to vanish. Balor's daughter then approached them and asked her father to have pity on the young man and to give him the cow.

'I'll tell you what I'll do,' said Balor to his daughter. 'Let you take the cow's halter! I will stand here in front of you, and the young man can stand behind you, and the person to whom you throw the halter can have the cow.'

Balor thought, of course, that the daughter would throw the halter to himself. She swung the halter above her head and threw it behind her. Gaibhde the Smith caught it; that meant that the cow was his once more!

'Daughter,' said Balor, 'from now on, I ordain that every woman in the world will have a crooked aim!'

And so they have, as every woman swings things over her shoulders before she throws them!

Gaibhde the Smith and the boy and the cow reached the mainland without any trouble.

'Meet me here on the strand nine months from tonight,' said the boy to Gaibhde, when they were parting.

Nine months from that night, Gaibhde the Smith went to the strand, and the boy was waiting for him in his small stone coracle.

'Sit into the coracle,' said the boy, 'and we'll go to Tory to see have we left anything behind us.'

Gaibhde jumped in and they never stopped until they reached Tory. The boy took Gaibhde on his back and they went in to the women. They found that Balor's daughter had given birth to a son, and each of the twelve waiting-women had a young daughter. The boy knotted a sheet around his waist, put the twelve female babies into it and fixed a bog-deal splinter through it to hold it tight. He took up Gaibhde the Smith's son between his two hands, and he and Gaibhde went down to the coracle. When they were close to the mainland, the boy pulled the splinter from the sheet over the sea, and let the twelve baby girls fall into the water.

'I place ye under *geasa* to be seals in the sea for ever more!' said he.

Gaibhde the Smith took his own son home, and the crying of the child kept him awake all night long. The child was restless through lack of food, and Gaibhde the Smith couldn't cure that! He went down to the strand next day, blaming himself for his own foolishness. It wasn't long till he saw the boy coming towards him in the coracle.

'How did the baby spend the night?' asked the boy.

'Badly, I can tell you!' said Gaibhde.

'Bring him down here and we'll take him back to Tory!' said the boy.

They never stopped till they reached Tory with the child.

'Go in to Balor now and tell him that your wife has died and left you with a young baby. Tell him that you have no milk for him and that you heard he had a crowd of young women, who had very little to do. Tell him that you would be very grateful if he took pity on the child and allowed the women to rear him for a while.'

Gaibhde the Smith went to Balor and asked for what the boy had told him. Balor said that he had many women, but that none of them had breast-milk.

'Well,' said Gaibhde the Smith, 'my child has the gift of filling with milk the breasts of any woman to whom he is given!'

'That's the house up there where the women are!' said Balor. 'Take him up and let them have him!'

Gaibhde took the baby to the castle and gave the baby to each of the thirteen women in turn. Then in walked Balor.

'Of course, you didn't give the child to my own daughter?' asked Balor.

'I never yet passed over one woman for another!' said Gaibhde the Smith. 'Your daughter was the first woman I met.'

'Well, he won't be short of breast-milk now, anyway!' said Balor.

Gaibhde the Smith left the child behind in Tory and went back to the mainland with the boy, very happy and contented. Before they parted, the boy asked Gaibhde to meet him on the strand in a year's time, when they would go to Tory for the child. When the year was up, they took the child home from Tory; he was three times as big as any other child of his age would be. He continued to grow until he was sent to school, and he could learn more than three other children together! When he was seven years old, there wasn't a boy, large or small, in the school that he couldn't beat. The years went by until he grew to be a man.

One night, he was invited to a wedding-feast in the townland. Balor had two men named Maol and Mullogue in Tory, and whenever one of Balor's tenants got married, these two would arrive to demand the right to spend the wedding-night with the bride. That was Balor's law, and it would be wrong to break it. Gaibhde the Smith wasn't long at the wedding-feast when he caught sight of the two Tory men coming towards the house. He asked who they were and was told why they were coming.

'I'm going to put a stop to that law,' said he.

He rushed to the door and took by the throat the first of the pair who put his nose inside the threshold. He knocked him to the ground, and then caught hold of the other fellow and dragged him down on top of his companion. He killed both of them. The feast was very pleasant after that, as everybody was glad that the pair had been got rid of. News of their deaths was carried to Balor in Tory, and he was mad with rage.

'My grandfather will come here to the mainland soon,' said the son of Gaibhde the Smith, 'and he'll murder someone!'

He cut down a large tree and left it at the high-water mark at the place where Balor would come ashore. Balor had only one eye, a poisonous one at the back of his head, and he didn't notice the tree when he jumped out of his boat. He stumbled over the tree and, in his rage, he began to hew it to pieces with his sword until all his strength had gone. His grandson, the son of Gaibhde the Smith, and he then attacked each other, and Balor pursued his opponent, as he fell back, until they reached Glenveagh. At last, the grandson got the chance of pushing his sword into Balor's poisonous eye at the back of his head. That was the only way by which he could be killed.

'You are my grandson, however you came into the world!' said the dying Balor.

'I am, grandfather.'

'Come near me and place your head under the tear that is dropping from my eye,' said Balor, 'and I will make you the greatest warrior in all the world.'

The grandson pushed a large green stone underneath the eye.

'That's my head now, grandfather,' said he.

Balor let the poisonous tear from his eye fall on the stone. The stone melted under it, and the tear dug a hole into the earth. Lough Veagh now lies in that hole.

When Balor was dead, there was no mourning for him on account of his bad laws. Gaibhde the Smith and his son went to Tory, and Gaibhde married Balor's daughter. They had a fine, quiet, peaceful life from that time on.

2 The Fate of the Sons of Uisneach

THIS TALE IS ONE OF THE 'Three Sorrows of Storytelling' in Irish tradition (the other two being 'The Fate of the Children of Tuireann' and 'The Fate of the Children of Lir'). It belongs to the Ulster cycle of storytelling. The earliest mention of the tale is found in a manuscript dating from the ninth century, and the present version is probably derived from a fifteenth century form of the tale. Thus, the story has been current in oral tradition for a fairly long time. It has been recorded in Ulster and Connacht in Ireland, as well as in Scotland, while it is of comparatively rare occurrence in Munster.

The unfolding of the tragic story hinges on the prophecy that the child, Deirdre, will bring bloodshed and sorrow in her train. Her desertion of her elderly suitor, Conchobhar, king of Ulster, and her elopement with Naoise, one of the sons of Uisneach, who are officers in the king's army, are basic themes in the tale, and are found in the literary tradition of Europe (the story of Tristan and Iseult, and that of Diarmaid and Gráinne in the present volume).

One day Manannán was sitting in his house. There was nobody present except his wife, who was soon to bear a child. As she crossed the floor, the child in her womb spoke three times.

'Ah, you rip!' shouted Manannán to the unborn child. 'Things won't happen as you foretell. It would be sinful that even a quarter of that number should die because of you. When you come into this world, your length of life will be only as long as it will take me to drown you!'

'God preserve us!' said his wife. 'What's that you are saying and why are you talking like that?'

'I'll tell you that,' said Manannán. 'You are bearing a baby girl in your womb, and she said just now that two-thirds of the men of Ireland, one-third of the men of Scotland, and the three sons of Uisneach will die because of her. That's why I said that I myself would drown her as soon as she came into the world, rather than that so many warriors should be killed on account of her.'

Shortly afterwards, the woman had labour pains. Manannán was there when the child, Deirdre, was born; such a beautiful child had never before been born. All that Manannán did was to jump to his feet, take hold of a large osier basket, put the baby into it, and cover her over so that she wouldn't be seen when he was drowning her. Out the door he rushed with the basket. Who should happen to come in at that moment but the High King of Ireland, and he asked Manannán where he was going with the basket. Manannán replied that he was going out to drown young pups that he did not want to keep.

'Lay down the basket till I have a look at them,' said the king.

Manannán laid down the basket reluctantly. The king raised the cloth that was covering Deirdre and said that no more beautiful woman had ever been born than the child would become, if she lived.

'Why are you going to drown her?' asked the king.

'I'll tell you that,' said Manannán. 'Two-thirds of the men of Ireland, one-third of the men of Scotland and the three sons of Uisneach will die because of her.'

'Do you know what you'll do?' said the king—he was a very young man. 'Give her to me and I will take her to my palace. I will build a very fine court for herself and for the women who will be minding her, and I will make sure that she will never lay eyes on any man except on myself, nor will she know any other man lives except myself. Then when she has grown to womanhood, I will marry her.'

'All right,' said Manannán. 'Take her away.'

The king took her away in the basket, very proud of her beauty. He built a very fine court for her, and, as for nurses, there was no shortage; and she had hundreds. No man, but women only, were to be admitted to the court. And no day passed without the king coming to see her, until she was sixteen years of age.

One fine day she was up on top of the court. It was wintertime and heavy snow covered the ground. Down below her was a butcher, with a big sledge and knife, killing bullocks. Deirdre watched him from the top of the court. When the butcher had killed the bullocks, he and his men dressed the meat and went off home. Deirdre was looking down from the window and she saw three black ravens drinking the blood which had flowed from the animals. Deirdre looked at the heavy snow, at the three ravens and at the blood. After a while, she spoke to her nurse.

'Oh, lord of the world!' said she. 'If there were a man whose skin was as white as the snow, whose two cheeks were as red as the blood, and whose hair was as black as the ravens! Do you think there is in the world a man like that?'

The nurse laughed and said that there was one such man.

'Do you think I could see him?' asked Deirdre. 'Who is he?'

'His name is Naoise, one of the sons of Uisneach. His skin is as white as that snow you see, his two cheeks are as red as that blood and his hair is dark as the raven.'

'Oh, what a pity that I can't see him! Where does he live?' asked Deirdre.

'He's a high general over the king's soldiers,' said the nurse, 'and his two brothers, Aill and Ardán, are almost as fine as he is.'

'God help me!' cried Deirdre. 'Is there any way at all in the world that I can see them?'

'I'll tell you how you can see them,' said the nurse. 'The king will be coming here to see you tomorrow, and when he comes, you must pretend to be in bad humour. Don't give him much talk at all! He'll ask you what's wrong with you today beyond any other day. Tell him that you're angry with him because he keeps you confined here, without seeing a person or animal since you came. Tell him he doesn't even let his army and soldiers out on the street for you to look at. If he promises that he'll do that for you,' said the nurse, 'he'll do it tomorrow, for he won't break his word to you. If they pass this way tomorrow, Ardán and his men will lead the way. But you mustn't take a liking to him on any account! Aill will be next, with his men, but, for the life of you, you mustn't fall in love with him. Naoise will follow, and he's the finest man in the world. His skin is white as the snow, his two cheeks are as red as blood and his hair is dark as the raven.'

The nurse had barely finished speaking when the king came in. Deirdre took no notice of him, so he spoke to her and asked what was wrong. She told him not to be bothering her.

'What's wrong with you?' asked the king.

'I have good cause to be angry with you,' said Deirdre, 'for 'tis little you have shown to me since the day you brought me here. You haven't had enough care or thought for me to get your army to march past the court to let me have a look at them.'

'If that's all that you're complaining about,' said the king, 'you'll see them after noon tomorrow passing the court. We're going to get married the day after that.'

She burst out laughing at the joy of getting married to him, as it were. She was in great good humour for the rest of the evening, and the king was delighted. He left her then and went home.

Next day when mid-day was at hand, Deirdre and her nurse went to the top of the court. They weren't long there when Deirdre saw the finest man that she had ever seen, a warrior general, and almost three hundred men following him. When he came near the court, Deirdre cried:

'Oh, lord, has such a fine man ever been born?'

'You trickster of all women, beware that you don't fall in love with him!', warned the nurse. 'He's not half as fine as his brother, Aill, who is coming next.'

It wasn't long until Deirdre saw the other brother, Aill, coming with his own men.

'Oh, lord!' cried Deirdre, 'has as fine a man as that ever been born till now, or ever again?'

'You trickster of all women!' said the nurse. 'Don't give any love to him, for he's not near as fine a man as his eldest brother, Naoise, who is to come yet.'

She let Aill pass by. It wasn't long until she saw Naoise approaching and, of course, the moment she laid eyes on him, she almost died with love for him. His skin was as white as the snow, his two cheeks were as red as blood and his hair as black as the raven. She wrote a note, and when Naoise was passing underneath the window where she was, she threw down the letter and it touched Naoise's head. He looked up, and when he saw Deirdre, he fell in love with her. She had asked him in the note to come to the court that night and she would throw herself down from the window, six storeys up, and risk her life in the attempt.

Naoise and his men went to wherever the king had ordered them. The day passed and night came. Naoise went to where his brothers, Aill and Ardán, were, and they all agreed to go to Deirdre's court later that night.

'Even though, I suppose,' said Naoise, 'that there will be great war and murder between the king and ourselves tomorrow on account of Deirdre.'

At midnight they came to the court and were beneath Deirdre's window at the top. She was at the window, expecting them, her body extended out as far as her waist. As soon as she saw them below, she threw herself out. It was no trouble to the three sons of Uisneach to jump six storeys upwards and support her with the palms of their hands. They brought her down unhurt and took her back to their quarters. As soon as day broke, news reached the king that Deirdre had gone off with Naoise, son of Uisneach. He roused his soldiers and ordered them to kill the sons of Uisneach. By midday, the sons of Uisneach, unaided, had slain two-thirds of the men of Ireland. Fighting ended for that day, and Deirdre went home with the three sons of Uisneach. That night, Naoise, Deirdre's lover, spoke:

'Wouldn't it be sad for us to go fighting again tomorrow,' said he, 'and not leave a man, who deserves to be called a man, alive in Ireland?'

'It would be better for us,' said his brother, Aill, 'to leave Ireland altogether and go to some other kingdom for a while in the hope that his anger will pass from the king and we may return.'

'Better for us to move immediately and go to Scotland,' said Ardán.

'We'll do that,' said Naoise, 'and we'll seek refuge on top of the highest hill in Scotland. No living person will know that we're there.'

They went to Scotland and built a little house on top of the highest hill there, in a lonely place. They spent a half-year there. Naoise and Deirdre used not to leave the house at all, but Aill and Ardán used to go each day to the town for food for them all. One fine day when the sun was shining brightly, Naoise and Deirdre went out into the sunshine at the gable of the house and were conversing. They noticed nothing until they caught sight of four gentlemen approaching them. One of them was the son of the King of Scotland, and he fell in love with Deirdre when he saw her. He asked her would she marry him and go off with him. Deirdre replied that indeed she would not marry him; she said that she was already married and that Naoise was her husband. The king's son went home, dying with love for Deirdre. He spent the whole night gathering his army to send them to the hill to take Deirdre away by force. When day came, the soldiers went to the hill. Deirdre and the three brothers were in the house. An officer entered and asked Deirdre to accompany him. Naoise ordered him to leave, saying that he would not get the woman as she was his own wife.

'That means war then,' said the officer.

The fighting began, and before much of the day was spent, one-third of the men of Scotland lay dead at the hands of the sons of Uisneach. News spread through the kingdoms of the world then that they had killed one-third of the men of Scotland in a few hours of daylight. The King of Ireland heard this and asked an old, wise man that he had, how he might try to put the sons of Uisneach to death.

'I'll tell you how,' said the wise man. 'You must build a court with a roof of lead, and when it is roofed, cover the lead inside and outside with lime-white thatch, as well as all the rooms. When you have the court built, store a lot of firewood nearby. Send word to the four of them in Scotland then, saying that you have built a fine court for them, and that there will be great friendship between you and them again, as there was before, if they come to Ireland. When they come and are asleep at night, you will get some of your soldiers to draw the firewood about the court and set it afire. The lead will melt above them and they will be burned alive.'

The king built the court, and when it was ready he sent for them, asking them to return to Ireland, saying that he had a place made for them, and that there would be nothing but friendship between them for ever more.

They returned to Ireland, and the king had great welcome for them, moryah. He made a gift of the court to them, and they kept company with one another until midnight. They then went to bed and fell asleep, the three sons of Uisneach and Deirdre. The king and his men set fire to the wood around the court. When it was alight and blazing, the lead began to melt. Deirdre was the first to scream when the molten lead touched her. The three sons of Uisneach did not notice the burning at all, for they had the gift of safety from fire. They jumped up, and the three of them took hold of Deirdre and surrounded her to keep the lead from her. She was screaming and wailing. The three of them jumped upwards, holding Deirdre safe between them, and went out through the roof. They landed about a quarter-mile from the court, holding Deirdre unharmed.

The three of them were blinded, however, for the lead had touched their eyes. When the king saw that they were blinded, he ordered his soldiers to attack and kill them. The three fought against the king's army and killed most of them, except a few who ran aside in terror. The sons of Uisneach were wild with anger and fury, and blind into the bargain. Ardán and Aill met each other and, in their anger and blindness did not know what they were doing. Deirdre was wailing and shouting to them that they were killing each other. But their fury was so great that they did not understand what she was telling them, and Aill killed his brother, Ardán. When that had happened, Naoise and Aill came together. Deirdre was screaming as loudly as she could, telling each who the other was. But so great was their anger that they did not know what she meant. Naoise killed Aill. He had no one else to fight against then.

'You have done an evil deed,' said Deirdre. 'Aill has killed Ardán and you have killed Aill.'

'If I have,' said Naoise, 'I'll never kill anyone again.'

He held his sword and drove it into his breast. The three brothers were then dead.

The sun never shone on a more pitiful sight than Deirdre lamenting over them, from one to one. She spent two hours crying over the body of her own husband, Naoise. She then cried for an hour over Aill, and when she had done that, she spent another hour crying over Ardán. Great was her heartbreak and sorrow for them.

The King of Ireland came towards her.

'You're mine now in spite of the world,' said he.

'I'm not,' said Deirdre. 'I'll have no man since I lost my husband, Naoise.'

The king walked towards her, and he and two or three of his men seized her. He forced her into his coach. As they were crossing a bridge, she threw herself headlong out of the coach, and her skull was fractured into bits. That was her choice, rather than be the wife of the king.

The sons of Uisneach had three gifts: no weapons could kill them; the sea could not drown them; and no fire could burn them.

That's the way I heard that story being told by my own father, William Burke of Aird Mhór. The dear blessing of God and of the Church on the souls of the dead, and may all who are here be seven thousand times better off a year from today!

3 Diarmaid and Gráinne

THE FIANNA IN TRADITION WERE bands of roving warriors and hunters, who were under the command of their leader Finn mac Cool (Fionn mac Cumhail), and were called upon by the King of Ireland to defend the country when danger threatened from outside. Hundreds of tales, in prose and verse, about their exploits and adventures, were more popular than the tales of the Ulster Cycle. The characteristic qualities of the Fianna were summarised in the saying, ' cleanliness of heart, strength of arm and fulfilment of promises'. Tales of the Fianna were well-known in Gaelic-speaking Scotland, as in Ireland.

Like the preceding tale of The Fate of the Sons of Uisneach, the main theme is centred on the desertion by the heroine of her elderly suitor for a younger lover, the pursuit of the eloping lovers and the death of the hero, Diarmaid. The tale of Diarmaid and Gráinne was mentioned in a saga-list of the tenth century, and the earliest full manuscript version dates from the fourteenth century.

Many dolmens throughout Ireland were popularly known as Leapacha Dhiarmada agus Ghráinne (Beds of Diarmaid and Gráinne), where the lovers were said to have rested during their flight.

One day when the Fianna were hunting on the mountains of Ireland, they arrived at the palace of King Cormac mac Airt. He had a daughter named Gráinne, and it was said that she was as beautiful a woman as was to be found in Ireland at that time. Finn mac Cool was a widower just then, and his one wish in the world was to get Gráinne as his wife.

As the Fianna were crossing the ford towards the king's palace, a fairy appeared before them and said:

' Go back, go back, Finn mac Cool!
Don't go to mac Airt's house!
If you get Gráinne, the king's young daughter,
It won't be for your benefit!'

This didn't discourage Finn or his men. They went on to the

palace, and Finn told Cormac why he had come. Cormac heartily consented to give him his daughter. At that time, Finn was well known all over Ireland, and both high and low had great esteem for him.

A night was fixed for the betrothal and a day for the marriage. Cormac invited all his own court, and Finn and his Fianna also came for the festivities. On the night of the betrothal, when all had arrived at the palace, Cormac went out and locked all the gates around it. It was as fine a night of celebration as had ever been held in Ireland. Around midnight, Gráinne got to her feet and said that she had not yet handed out a drink, and it was time to do so now. She ordered a servant to go out to the room where the whiskey was stored and to bring in a certain keg. The servant did so and when he had brought in the keg, Gráinne took up a goblet and filled it with whiskey. She gave it to drink to the man who sat at Diarmaid O Duibhne's right hand and passed it around the circle until it came back, empty, to Diarmaid.

'Diarmaid,' said she, 'it looks as if I did not wish to give you anything to drink!'

'I wouldn't hold that against you, Gráinne,' said Diarmaid. 'I have had plenty to drink already.'

'Well, there's more where that drink came from,' said Gráinne.

She took the goblet and went out to the whiskey-room. She delayed there for a while, and when she returned, everybody in the room had fallen fast asleep, except Diarmaid O Duibhne.

'Gentle Diarmaid of the brown hair,' said Gráinne,
'Most comely of body from head to feet,
Come away with me to the edge of the waves!
You, not Finn, are my choice!'

'I assure you, Gráinne,' said Diarmaid, 'that I would be glad to have you as wife in honour of the king. Many's the fine day I hunted with him over moors and mountains, enjoying ourselves. But Finn mac Cool is the great leader of the Fianna, and we'll never hear the end of it, if you and I elope together!'

'That's the way it will have to be, Diarmaid,' said she.

'Don't say any more,' said Diarmaid.

They left the palace and found all the gates closed.

'There's a secret way out,' said Gráinne.

'If I get out of here,' said Diarmaid, 'I'll go as a warrior would, and if I can't do that, I'll stay here.'

He went to the main gate in front of the palace. He then

stepped back a few paces, jumped and went clear out across the gate. Gráinne did the same. They went to a stable that was outside the walls, harnessed two horses to a coach and drove off till they came to the edge of a river. Gráinne said that they could go no further. They untied the horses, and Diarmaid led one of them through the river and left it grazing at the other side. They walked up a small, nice hillock, and sat down to talk about the times that had gone and what lay ahead of them. Then they both fell asleep.

When the Fianna awoke in Cormac's palace and found Diarmaid and Gráinne missing, Finn chewed his thumb of knowledge and learned that the pair were asleep on the hill. He ordered his men to get up and go in pursuit of them immediately. They set out, Finn at their head, and went straight to where the pair were asleep. When they came within shouting distance of them, Finn said that they had never yet killed a bird or a beast, let alone a person, without giving them a chance of escaping or defending themselves.

'Diarmaid and Gráinne must get that chance too,' said Finn.

He shouted loudly to the pair to defend themselves. They woke up and found that they were in danger. Gráinne saw that they were in trouble and she began to cry.

'Sit up here on my arm!' said Diarmaid.

He drew his sword from its scabbard and faced for where the Fianna were thickest. He hewed a passage through them and hid on the other side—it was said of Diarmaid that he was as swift as a hare in a mountain glen! The Fianna had to return home empty-handed. Diarmaid and Gráinne knew that they would be pursued again the next night. When night came, they made their bed on the mountain lying on sand from the sea-shore. Finn chewed his thumb again and learned that the fugitives were asleep on the sand of the sea-shore. He ordered his men to search the sea-shore, but he did not accompany them. The Fianna searched the shore, but returned home without finding anything. Diarmaid and Gráinne knew that they would be pursued again the next night. They took heather from the mountain and made a bed of it on the sand-hills at the shore. Finn chewed his thumb again and learned that they were asleep on the heather of the mountain. He ordered his men to search the mountain, but it was all in vain; they came home as they had left, empty-handed.

Finn suspected that his men were deceiving him, so he sent a request to the King of Scotland to send his best men to Ireland to

capture one of the Fianna, Diarmaid O Duibhne. No sooner had
Finn sent this message to Scotland than Diarmaid and Gráinne
learned about it. The Fianna spent some time watching the
harbours and coast of Ireland, waiting for the Scotsmen to land,
but when they were slow in coming, the Fianna went inland.

Diarmaid and Gráinne were sitting one day on a mountain-side
in County Down, when they saw a sailing-ship approaching. They
knew that it was carrying the Scotsmen. When the ship came to
the shore, Diarmaid and Gráinne went down to meet it, and the
captain asked them did they know where Finn mac Cool lived.
Diarmaid said that they did, and that Finn had sent him to meet
them and to teach them some feats of prowess, without which
they would never be able to capture the man they were after.

' 'Tis too late to start teaching you today,' said Diarmaid. ' Be
ready tomorrow morning, and I'll be here!'

When Diarmaid arrived at the ship next morning, the Scotsmen
were ready. He brought them to a field near the shore, at the top of
which was a small wood. He cut two poles in the wood and stood
them near each other in the field. He then placed his sword, with
its edge upwards, on top of the poles. He drew back a few paces
and jumped clear over the sword.

' I would like to know now,' said Diarmaid, ' which man of you
can imitate that.'

The first Scotsman that tried the jump came down on the sword
and was cut in two. The same thing happened to the second, and so
on until the bodies of thirty of them were lying in a heap beyond
the sword.

' Enough of you have died today,' said Diarmaid, ' without being
able to do what I did! We'll try another trick tomorrow.'

The Scotsmen returned to their ship that night, and Diarmaid
and Gráinne slept soundly. Next morning, Diarmaid went to the
ship again, and the Scotsmen were waiting for him. There was an
empty barrel lying beside the quay, and Diarmaid took it on his
shoulders to the top of a small, green hill. There he filled the
barrel with stones and let it roll down the slope, while he himself
danced on top of the barrel all the way to the shore. He then
emptied the barrel of stones and took it to the top of the hill
again. He filled it with stones once more, and asked the Scotsmen
to do the trick. When one of them attempted to dance on the
barrel as it rolled downhill, it turned and he was killed. And so
it went on until thirty-four of them lost their lives in the same way.

'I see,' said Diarmaid, 'that not a man among you is able to imitate me. I am the man ye came to Ireland to capture. Now I am ready to fight ye or to allow ye to return home as quickly as ye came.'

'I think we had better go back home,' said the captain.

'Very well,' said Diarmaid.

The Scotsmen went back to the ship, hoisted the sails and set out for their own country. Diarmaid and Gráinne spent a season in every part of Ireland. It was a hard, uncomfortable life for both of them: the king's daughter who had been reared in a palace, with girls and women attending on her with the best of food, and one of the Fianna, who also had got the best of food and had thrown the worst of it over his shoulder. Still, they were satisfied with the way things were. One day when they were seated on a mountain-side in Sligo, they heard the baying of hounds approaching.

'They sound very much like the hounds of Finn,' said Diarmaid.

He went to the top of the mountain and saw an enraged boar coming towards him, pursued by a pack of eager hounds.

'If I were with Finn mac Cool today,' said Diarmaid, 'that boar wouldn't go very far.'

He ran down the side of the mountain and faced the boar. He jumped on its back and slowed it down. When the boar heard the hounds baying at its heels, it turned its head and took a full bite out of Diarmaid's thigh. Blood poured from the gash; Diarmaid grew dizzy and fell to the ground. Gráinne ran to him, but could do nothing, only look at him. At last the Fianna came up. Finn ordered one of his men to fetch a plaster for the wound, but when he brought it, Diarmaid was already dead. They waked and buried him, and when the last of the clay was thrown on the grave, Finn said:

'Well, Gráinne,' said he, 'you left me and went off with Diarmaid. You have now lost him. Are you willing to have me as your husband?'

Gráinne agreed. The two of them got married but, if they did, they spent an unhappy life till they too went to the grave.

4 Finn and the Big Man

SOME OF THE MORE HEROIC tales about the Fianna have as their theme either their defence of Ireland against foreign invaders (as in *Cath Fionntrá*: The Battle of Ventry) or else their adventures in a foreign land. The following tale is also centred mainly on Ventry in West Kerry but is concerned mainly with the visit of a stranger from a foreign kingdom to request Finn, leader of the Fianna, to accompany him to save a princess who is to be devoured by a sea-monster, as in the Perseus story from Greek classical literature. While Finn does ultimately slay the monster, that part of the narrative is but an incident in the whole tale, which is mostly concerned with Finn's cleverness in avoiding recognition by the visitor and the manner in which he discovers how the foreign invaders may be overcome.

Finn mac Cool was living in the parish of Ventry in West Kerry in times gone by. He built a strong fortress and a fine castle there, and the castle is plainly to be seen there to the present day, as lofty and as firm as it was the day 'twas built. And why wouldn't it be? It is said the blood of cattle was used to wet the mortar for the walls.

Finn and the Fianna used to stay there when they were in that of Kerry. One day Finn was in his boat alone outside Ventry Harbour; the sun was shining gently down on him and the tide was out. Finn was seized with an unnatural desire to eat a handful of limpets. He went ashore and got a piece of stone and started to collect the shell-fish, and when he had filled a bag of them he went home. He collected some firewood and splinters of timber—there was plenty of that there in those days—and made a fire and started to roast the limpets. He was sitting on his haunches by the fire, roasting and chewing. When he gave a glance out towards the mouth of the harbour, he saw coming towards him a skiff, with one mast and one sail of purple colour. There was no one on board except a huge warrior. Finn took fright.

'My shame and reproach!' said he. 'I'm caught at last and

disgraced, a man like me to be roasting limpets on a little fire like this at this hour of day!'

He did his best to hide the limpets and throw them aside so that the huge warrior who was coming ashore would not see the shells or the limpets or notice what he was doing. But the stranger was too near for that.

'I place myself under heavy *geasa*,' said Finn, 'that nobody will ever again see me gathering limpets or roasting them.'

It wasn't long till the great warrior on board the skiff stuck the point of his sword into the deck and gave a mighty leap to land. He walked up to where Finn was, and they saluted each other.

'Tell me, my good man,' said the warrior, 'where here do Finn mac Cool and his men live?'

'They live above there,' said Finn. 'What business have you with Finn?'

'Isn't it inquisitive you are, you brat,' said the warrior. 'Who are you?'

'I'm a cow-herd,' said Finn. 'I work for Finn mac Cool, and my orders are not to let anyone pass me by without finding out what he wants, and I must bring an account of him to Finn and his men.'

'Very well,' said the big man. 'What kind of men are the Fianna? They have a great name as strong, active warriors.'

'So they are,' said Finn. 'They live up to their name.'

'Show me the way to their house,' said the warrior.

'I won't yet,' said Finn, 'till I find out what kind of a fellow you are and why you came here.'

'I'm a warrior from the Land of the Big Men. The king sent me here to ask Finn mac Cool to go with me to his kingdom to kill a monster that's under a spell in a lake there. She has to get the daughter of a king and queen to devour once every seven years, and now she's demanding the king's daughter. He sent me to bring Finn with me to kill the monster, since there is a prophecy that Finn mac Cool can kill her.'

'That may be,' said Finn, 'but Finn and his men won't go with you as easily as that.'

'I don't want his men,' said the warrior. 'All I want is Finn himself.'

'Finn won't go with you, for his men won't let him,' said Finn.

'They'll have to let him go with me,' said the big warrior. 'I have all kinds of magic powers: water cannot drown me or fire burn me, and no weapon can wound me.'

'That's what you say,' said Finn, 'but how can I know that it's true?'

'I'll prove to you that it's true,' said the big man. 'Come with me down this way, and put me under the water for an hour. Then you'll know whether water can drown me.'

Down they went to the little inlet of the sea that was near them. The big man stripped off his clothes, and down he went under the water. Finn took care to catch him by the head and keep him under the water, lest any puff of wind would help him to breathe, and didn't let him come to the surface for an hour or more.

'You're well drowned by this time,' said Finn to himself.

Up rose the big man as lively and active as he had ever been.

'You're a wonderful warrior, indeed,' said Finn. 'But how will I find out that fire won't burn you?'

'You'll find that out too,' said the big man. 'There's no shortage of firewood here around us. We'll kindle a fire, and when it will be red-hot, you can throw it on top of me.'

'Very well,' said Finn.

The two of them collected a huge pile of wood and set it afire. When it was blazing red, the big man stripped off his clothes and stretched himself face downwards over the fire. Finn didn't neglect to throw every thick, red-hot piece of wood that he could lay hands on on top of him to burn him alive. But there wasn't a groan or a cry of pain from the big man, nor was there any sign of burning or scalding on him in spite of the huge fire that was sizzling around him.

'You must think that I'm well burned by now,' said the big man after an hour had passed.

'I've always heard it said,' said Finn, 'that the greatest heat is at the end of a fire. Wait till the fire is dying down; 'tis then 'twill be hottest of all.'

Finn kept him down under the fire for another while, but it didn't matter at all. The big man rose up as hale and well as he had ever been.

'Does that satisfy you?' asked the big man.

'But how will I know that weapons won't hurt or kill you?' asked Finn.

'You'll know it this way,' said the big man. 'Take this sword and use it on me any way you wish. Strike me wherever you like!'

'Your sword wouldn't suit me,' said Finn, 'but I have a small rusty sword of my own here, which I use to pick meat from bones when I'm sitting down here herding the cattle. I think I'll use that.'

Finn took hold of his own sword and flashed it around his head. He then attacked the big man with the blade across his two shin-bones and knocked a heavy groan out of him. The big man rubbed his two shins to ease the pain.

'Well, if the Fianna are as strong as you are,' said the big man, 'you may well boast of them. When you'll grow to be a man, you'll have a strong blow, seeing that I felt your stroke even now.'

'But I'm only like a child in comparison with Finn mac Cool and his men!' said Finn.

'Will you direct me to their house now?' asked the big man.

'I will,' said Finn. 'Go over that way!'

Finn directed the big man by a roundabout way, and he himself ran by every short-cut to be at the house ahead of him. Gráinne Bharóid, their house-servant, was getting the dinner ready in the kitchen when Finn arrived.

'Give over your cooking,' said Finn. 'There's a giant warrior coming here to the castle, and no telling what he'll do. I'll get into this old box and let you pretend that I'm a baby. If he asks any questions, tell him that I'm not yet a year old, to see can we by any means get him to leave the house.'

Finn got into the box and kept talking to Gráinne.

'If he asks you what kind of amusement the Fianna have after their dinner,' said Finn, 'tell him that they try to pull up that big boulder outside there and throw it like a finger-stone over the house; then they rush to the other side of the house and catch the boulder behind their knees and throw it back again. When he hears that, he might be in a hurry to leave the house.'

Finn was lying in a big box at the side of the kitchen, with an old blanket twisted about him, and the woman was pretending to be rocking it like a cradle when in walked the warrior. They saluted each other.

'It looks as if this is the house of Finn mac Cool,' he said.

''Tis indeed,' said Gráinne.

'Where is he himself?' asked the big man.

'Himself and his men are out hunting and they aren't likely to be home for a while yet,' said she.

'I'll have to return to my own country so,' said the big man.

'I can't help that,' said Gráinne. 'You won't be able to meet Finn for another fortnight or maybe a month.'

She placed food and drink in front of him and he ate and drank his fill. He then went outside the house.

'Why have the Fianna only one door in this castle?' he asked. 'What do they do when there's a great wind and bad weather blowing in through that door?'

'Oh,' said she, 'they just catch the door and twist the house around so that the door is always on the sheltered side.'

'They must be strong men,' said the warrior.

'They are that,' said Gráinne.

'Have they any pastime after their dinner?' asked the big man.

'They have,' said she. 'There's a big boulder outside there, and the most I see them doing is casting it over the house and catching it behind their knees and throwing it back again.'

The big man went over to the huge boulder. It hadn't been stirred for as long as anyone could remember, but the big man lifted it up, with the dint of witchcraft and magic, and threw it with his hand across the wall that was there. He rushed after it and tried to catch it behind his knees as it fell, but the boulder tore off every inch of the skin of the backs of his knees, and small wonder! He came back into the house again, and his heart full of evil and mischief. He had made up his mind to kill the woman's baby in the box.

'What age is that child you have in the cradle?' he asked.

'He isn't a full year yet, my good man,' said she.

The big man went over, intending to put his finger into the baby's mouth to find out whether he had any teeth or was he older than she had said. If he did, Finn was ready for him. When he felt the finger in his mouth, he bit off the part of it that was inside his teeth, and let the big man pull away what was left of it. The big man let a mighty roar of pain out of him.

'I can promise you that that youngster has good teeth already,' said he.

'That's no surprise,' said the woman. 'The children of the Fianna have teeth when they are born.'

'I'll go home to my own country,' said the big man, 'and I'll bring back with me a large host of men that will defeat the Fianna. Then I'll be able to bring Finn mac Cool away with me.'

He went off out of the house and left the pair of them there. No sooner had he gone than Finn jumped out of the cradle.

'More bad luck to you!' said he, looking out after the big man. 'You're off now with four fingers, and the other's in my mouth! I have at least that much satisfaction out of you!'

The big man made off his own country, the Land of the Big Men, and Finn was making his own plans at home, without telling anyone what was in his mind. Nobody was told why the big man had come. When Finn was ready he called to him his young dog, Bran, and went down to where his skiff, the White Swan, was at anchor. He gave her a push and he and Bran jumped on board. Then he raised his sails of white, fine canvas, and never stopped until he reached the Land of the Big Men. He brought his skiff into the strand, and moored her for a year and a day, even though he might be away from her for only an hour. Himself and Bran walked about on the strand for a while. The big man's house was above the edge of the harbour, but neither he nor his family nor anybody else was to be seen. They had all gone to the king to get ready to go to Ireland to bring back Finn mac Cool. But the big man's wife was at home and she saw a little boy walking on the strand. She was wondering who he was. She left the house and never stopped till she went to where Finn was.

'What brought you here, little boy?' she asked.

'The current carried me here, my lady,' said Finn.

'You're welcome,' said she. 'You'll keep me company when my husband and family have gone to Ireland. I'll take you home, and you'll take the place of one of my children until they come back to me. Come up to the house with me.'

She hauled Finn and his dog to the house and didn't leave thirst or hunger on them. Finn spent two, three or four days there with her in the court; himself and the wife of the big man had a good time together. One day Finn asked her was she married or where was her husband or family.

'I haven't seen anyone around the house,' said he.

'They are all away getting ready to go to Ireland to bring Finn mac Cool here, for the daughter of our king is to be devoured by a devilish serpent that's in a lake here, and no one can stop that until Finn mac Cool kills the monster.'

'Is that so?' asked Finn. 'Will they come back here before they leave?'

'They will,' said the woman. 'My eldest son promised to say goodbye to me.'

A few days later, the big man, his three sons and his followers came to bid goodbye to their mother. They were so eager for the journey that none of them took any notice of the little boy, Finn, in the house. He was terrified that the big man might recognise him, seeing that he had already been speaking to him. But the big man took no notice of him, and no wonder—he had other things on his mind. They bade goodbye to the woman, and off they went.

Next day, she and Finn were in the parlour of the palace, eating their dinner and chatting; she was asking him all the questions she could think of, and he was answering them as best he could.

'Did you ever hear what kind of men the Fianna are?' she asked.

'No, lady,' said Finn. 'I don't know anything about them; I never met them; all I have heard about them is that they are great men.'

'They must be,' said she, 'and I'd say that nothing good will come of this visit of my husband and family to them now.'

'I have always heard,' said Finn, 'that nobody or no warrior has ever defeated the Fianna of Ireland in fight or battle.'

'Well, my family will defeat them for they can never be killed,' said the woman.

'That's their only chance to come back alive from Ireland to you,' said Finn.

'They have magic protection,' said the woman. 'Do you see those three helmets hanging there on the wall in front of you? My three sons can never be killed until they see those three helmets in the hands of Finn mac Cool.'

'Then their death is far away from them,' said Finn. 'They'll never be killed.'

'Never, they can't be killed,' said the woman.

That was that! They kept on chatting and conversing, and Finn was very happy at the information he had got. The woman left him and went out.

'I won't be long,' said she.

She left Finn sitting on his chair, and he made good use of her absence from the room. He jumped up, snatched down the three helmets, tucked them inside his clothes and stole out of the house. No one saw him. He whistled for Bran, his dog, and left the place and never stopped until he reached the lake where the king's daughter was to be devoured by the serpent. He and the dog waited there for a couple of days, walking up and down. At sunrise on the third day, the lake swelled up, and the serpent blew a great blast of water out of her nostrils and lifted her head above the water.

'Small welcome to you here, ugly, malicious Finn of the limpets from Ireland!' said she. 'You'd be at home in your own house in Ireland a long time before I'd intrude on you!'

'Bad luck to you, you ugly monster!' said Finn. 'If you behaved yourself, I wouldn't have to come here to fight you at all!'

'You'll make a small bite and a lot of soup for me now,' said she.

'You may think that!' said Finn.

She blew a blast from her nostrils, and half of her body came on the dry strand towards Finn to swallow him into her maw in one gulp. But Finn was ready for her. He held his sword straight in front of her, and the blade went into her throat, and split her in two back as far as her gullet. That moment, his dog, Bran, leaped into her throat and tore her heart and liver with his teeth before Finn saw what she was doing. He had to cut open the monster's breast to let Bran free again.

'That's so much done!' said Finn. 'I have done well myself, but I'm afraid of what's happening at home in my absence.'

He left the dead monster there and never stopped till he reached the strand where his skiff was tied up. He set it afloat and he and Bran jumped on board. We have no account of him until he sailed into the mouth of Ventry Harbour. The Fianna were fighting there, not knowing where Finn had gone. They had no account of him. As he sailed into the harbour, he could hear the sound of the blows and the clashing of swords on the strand.

'I suppose there won't be a man alive before me,' said he.

He sailed in and jumped from the skiff as soon as its prow touched the strand. He walked up the strand, where the two hosts were fighting and slaughtering each other. He made his way through them until he came upon the three sons of the big man, and they killing Fianna all around them. He pulled the three helmets from his bosom, raised them on high in his right hand and gave a loud shout. As soon as the three great warriors saw the helmets in Finn's hand, their arms fell from them and they lost all their strength. The Fianna then continued to kill them and lay them low, so that the big man had very few of them alive to return home with him. At last Finn spoke to him.

'Big man,' said he, 'Finn mac Cool has done you a good turn! Go home now with the few men you have left, and be grateful that you have your own head on your shoulders on your journey!'

The big man and his men returned to their own country and were surprised to hear that Finn mac Cool had killed the serpent and had stolen the three helmets from the wall of the big man's house.

Nothing could stop Finn except the sea!

5 Youth, the World and Death

FINN MAC COOL, HIS SON, Oisín, and his grandson, Oscar, are mentioned in this tale of the Fianna, which has a rare allegorical character. No battles or individual combats, no challenges or voyages, no 'runs' or colourful, descriptive language occur. Rather is the tale a moral one, which illustrates the transient quality of Youth and the power which Death holds over all men.

Some other versions of the tale end with the granting of gifts of various kinds by the old man of the strange house to individual members of the Fianna.

One day in the olden times, Finn mac Cool and his men were hunting in the mountains of Donegal. They followed a hind deep into a mountain, but she escaped, in spite of them, and they lost sight of her. They were tired, so they sat down on a small, round, grassy hill. A thick fog descended upon them, which looked as if it were caused by magic.

'Well, men,' said Finn mac Cool, 'if this fog doesn't clear, we're in danger of being lost tonight amongst these mountains, without a house anywhere near us.'

Just then, out of the corner of his eye, he caught sight of a weak ray of light in the glen below them. He asked the twelve men who were with him could they see the light, but none of them could.

'Follow me,' said Finn, 'and we'll go towards the light to see if we can shelter in the house till morning.'

They went down into the glen, and when they came near the light, there appeared before them the nicest castle that they had ever seen. All the Fianna were surprised that such a beautiful castle should be in the midst of the mountains. When they went nearer, they found the door open. A huge fire was blazing on the hearth. Seated in the corner beside it was a stooped, grey-haired, old man; his hair hung down over his shoulders, and the end of his beard covered his two knees. When the Fianna entered, Finn asked the old man could they lodge there until morning. He replied that they could, if they behaved themselves; if not, they couldn't. They were very surprised at this, that an old man who had one foot in the grave should speak like that.

They sat down by the fire, expecting to have the best night ever of storytelling and conversation with the old man, but, instead of that, he hadn't a word to say, except to answer any question that was put to him. There was a ewe sheep tied behind the door, and after a while she slipped the noose from her neck, walked up the floor and stood in front of the fire. The old man asked the Fianna to get up and take the ewe down again and tie her to the door.

'Ye are more lively and active than I am,' said he.

Oisín got up and took the ewe by the horn, but she butted him with her head and knocked him flat on the floor. When Oscar caught her by the horn, she did the same to him. Finn was sitting with his back to the hob.

'Well, men,' said he, 'ye have often before caused me shame and made me do work that ye should do, but this is the greatest shame of all!'

He jumped up and tried to take hold of the ewe, body and bones, but she knocked him to the floor even more quickly than she had knocked Oisín and Oscar. The three of them went back to their seats. Then the old man got to his feet and, with the aid of his stick, went and took the ewe by the horn, led her down to the door and tied her without any trouble.

'Well, men,' said he, when he sat down again, 'I must say that ye are a poor lot! A few old women could have done that little job!'

After a while, Finn asked him could they have some food. He said that they could. He took his stick tapped on the door of a room near the corner where he sat, and asked the girl who was there to come and get supper for the Fianna. When the young woman opened the door of the room, her beauty took the sight from the eyes of the Fianna. As she walked down along the floor, Oscar took hold of her hand. She struck him a blow on the cheek with her free hand, and told him that he had had her before and thought little of her! Oscar and the rest of the Fianna thought this a very strange thing to say, as they were sure that they had never seen her before.

She prepared supper for them, and when it was ready, she asked them to sit down at the table. It was as fine a supper as they had ever eaten. When they had finished, she cleared the table and laid it for breakfast next morning. She then went back to the room. Soon afterwards, the old man said that there were six beds ready for them in a lower room, and two of them should sleep in each bed.

'I'm sure that ye are tired,' said he, 'and ye want to lie down after being hunting since morning.'

The twelve Fianna went down to the room and went to bed. There wasn't a word out of anybody until morning. When Finn saw the dawn breaking, he jumped out of bed and ordered his men to get up. The girl was up as early as they were and had as fine a breakfast as they had ever eaten ready for them. When they had finished, Finn stood up and thanked the old man for the welcome he had given them, and for the supper and bed and breakfast.

'Now, I have three questions to ask you,' said Finn, 'and I'd be very grateful for answers to them.'

'I'll do my best,' said the old man, 'and, if I can't, I'm not to blame.'

'When we came in here to you last night,' said Finn, 'I asked you could we get lodgings until the morning. You said that we could, if we behaved ourselves, and, if we didn't, we couldn't. We thought that a very strange answer from you, who has one foot in the grave and one out of it. We thought then that there was nothing to overcome twelve warriors like us in the whole of Ireland. And still, not a single man of us was able to take that small ewe sheep back to the door and tie her there, but you did it without any trouble! One of my men fell in love with that young woman who came down from the room, and the answer she gave him was that he had had her before and thought little of her. Neither he nor any of us can remember ever having seen her before.'

'Those are good questions,' said the old man. 'That young woman who came down from the room is Youth, and when ye had Youth, little ye thought of it! Ye often insulted and abused it wrongly, and it went away from ye for ever. That ewe sheep that came up from the door is the World, and the World will be too strong for ye, mighty as ye are. As for myself, I am Death, and I have everybody under my thumb!'

Finn turned to see what his men thought of these answers to his questions, and when he looked around again, he found himself and his men standing on the mountainside, with nothing to be seen but sheep and goats grazing nearby.

6 The Everlasting Fight

THE HERO IN THIS FINE TALE IS nameless in the present version, but he is known as Céatach in several others. Tales such as this, of the epic or heroic type, were told only in the Irish language and did not pass over at all into English at any stage. This may have been due to the colourful and difficult-to-translate language in which they were told. As in the present version, this exotic language was to be found in the 'runs' or rhetorics with which the tale began, and continued through descriptions of challenges, combats, and travel over land or sea. The 'runs' were more or less static passages of speech, which served two purposes: *(a)* to impress the audience and *(b)* to allow the storyteller, who had these 'runs' at the tip of his tongue, to rest while reciting them and concentrate on the portion of the tale that was to follow.

Quests on which the hero was sent from one place to another were rather repetitive, but added to the tension of the situation until it was ultimately eased at the end.

More than 150 versions of the tale of 'The Everlasting Fight' have been recorded in Ireland during the past thirty years.

For a discussion of the tale and for comment on the 'run' as a feature of heroic storytelling, see *Gaelic Folk-tales and Mediaeval Romances*, Alan Bruford, Dublin (1966), 182-209, 220-221.

It was long ago, and a long time ago it was. If I were alive then, I wouldn't be alive now. If I were, I would have a new story or an old one, or I mightn't have any story! Or I might have lost only my back teeth or my front teeth or the furthest back tooth in my mouth!

There was a warrior in Ireland long ago, and his occupation

was hunting and fowling on the hillside, listening to the baying of hounds and the clanging of chains, to the whistle of the man from the east and the call of the man from the west, and no sweeter to him would be the storm from the west across the lake than the coming of Conán Maol as he threw stones! One day when the warrior was hunting and fowling with his pack of hounds, he saw three men bearing a box like a coffin on their shoulders. He went towards them and stood in front of them to find out what they had in the box, but they weren't willing to tell him that or where they were taking it to. So he decided to take the box from them, if he were strong enough, and see what was in it. They attacked one another, and it wasn't long until he had beaten them badly and taken the box from them. He then opened it to see what was inside. It was a woman whose like he had never seen, so beautiful was she.

'I'm taking this woman with me,' said he, 'whether ye like it or not!'

'You're not!' said one of the men. 'We'll lose our heads rather than let you take her!'

'I'm taking her and cutting the heads off the three of you as well!' said the warrior.

One of the three was bolder than the other two, so the warrior drew a blow of his sword at him and severed one of his arms.

'Go off home now and take your arm with you!' said the warrior.

He took the woman home that evening and put her into a room until next day, when he intended to take her to a monk or a priest—whichever sort was there at that time—to get married. As soon as he got up next morning, he went to the room where he had left the woman, but she wasn't there. He didn't know where she had gone to, so he said to himself that he would never stop or stay until he found her, wherever in Ireland she might be. He set forth and kept on walking and travelling until the day was drawing to a close; until the white gelding was seeking the shade of the dock-leaf, though the dock-leaf wouldn't stand still for him; and until the sun had sunk into the earth and night was falling. He saw a light far away, and not near him, so he went towards it and entered a house. No sooner had he come in than the young woman for whom he was searching came down from a room. She smothered him with kisses and drowned him with tears, and then dried him with fine, silken towels and with her own hair. There wasn't a man anywhere she thought more of! The arm which he had severed from one of the three men the previous day was lying on a table at the other side of the room. It rose up from the table suddenly and struck him a painful blow on the jaw-bone.

'You wouldn't do that again, arm,' said the warrior, 'if I thought it worth my while to strike you back!'

'Well,' said the young woman, 'the three men who were carrying me yesterday when you took me from them are my three brothers, and when they come home here tonight, they'll kill me and they'll kill you, unless they promise me that they won't harm you. But I must hide you until I get that promise from them.'

She left him, and when he had eaten his supper, she hid him and told him about her brothers. They had to spend every day of their lives, she said, fighting against three waves of enemies, who wanted to take their land from them and banish them.

'My brothers kill them all every day,' said she, 'but they are alive next morning, ready to fight again! And since you cut the arm off one of them, it will take them longer each day to kill the enemy, and they will come home later in the evening.'

That was that! The three brothers came into the house later in the night and sat down to eat their supper. Each one of them said that all he asked for was to have revenge on the man who had cut off the arm of one of them. When they were seated at the table, eating, their sister didn't sit down with them to eat at all. They asked her why she wasn't eating.

'I won't ever eat anything again,' said she, 'unless ye promise me something.'

'We'll promise you anything in the world that we can,' they said, 'except to spare the man who cut the arm off our brother!'

'Ye must promise me whatever I ask for,' said she.

Well, rather than keep her from eating, they promised to do what she wanted, if she ate her food. When they had eaten their supper, she told them what she wanted and uncovered the warrior. Each of the three brothers rushed to attack him, but when they remembered their promise to their sister, not to kill or harm him, they sat down again. Next morning, as soon as they had eaten their breakfast, they got ready to leave the house. He asked them where they were going, and they told him about the three waves of enemies they had to fight each day of their lives.

'They are alive again next morning,' they told him, 'although we have been killing them for many years. If we didn't kill them every day, we would soon have to leave this place altogether.'

'I'll go with ye today to see what I can do,' said the warrior 'I should be able to do at least as well as the one of you that has lost his arm!'

'Stay at home today! Tomorrow will be soon enough for you,' they said.

'I won't,' said he. 'I'll go with ye today to see how these men that ye are killing every day can be alive again next morning.'

He went along with them, although they didn't want him to leave the house that day. They were very friendly towards him, in spite of the blame they had on him the previous day. They reached the place where the three waves of enemies were waiting for them, armed with swords and every kind of weapon they could get for the fight.

'Ye must sit down now,' said the warrior to the three brothers, 'until I see what I'm able to do against these.'

He made the three sit down. Then he seized his sword and started to cut off the heads of the enemies, and by the end of two hours, not one of them was alive! It used to take the three brothers the whole day and part of the night to do as much!

'Ye are to go home now,' he told the brothers, 'but I won't leave this place until I find out what is making them alive again every night.'

'You mustn't stay,' said the brothers. 'If you stay here and we go home, our sister will say that we killed you, and she will lose her mind.'

'I don't care,' said the warrior. 'I won't ever leave here until I find out what is making these dead alive again. Go home, and ye can come again tomorrow, if I don't return to the house.'

The three brothers went home, and the warrior remained watching the dead bodies. When night came, he threw heaps of them here and there and lay down between them. It was just midnight when he saw a hag approaching with a small pot in which there was a quill in her hand. She started to throw a dash with the quill of whatever was in the pot on the bodies, and hundreds of them rose up as well and strong and healthy as they had ever been. He kept watching her until she had sprinkled them a few times, and said to himself that, unless he stopped her in time, he would have plenty to do against her and the enemy, if they all came back to life! He attacked them, and it didn't take him long to kill all the men she had revived. Himself and the hag then attacked each other, and he found it harder to overcome her than the three waves of enemies he had killed the previous day. He knocked her down at last and was ready to cut off her head.

'I put *geasa* on you,' said the hag, 'never to stop or rest until you go to the King of the Bridge and tell him that you killed the Sow and her Litter!'

He cut off her head and set out to find the King of the Bridge. When he came to where he lived, he struck the challenge-pole. He didn't leave a foal in a mare, a calf in a cow, a kid in a she-goat, or a piglet in a sow that he didn't turn around nine times in their skins, with the dint of the blow. The King of the Bridge came out to him.

'I killed the Sow and her Litter tonight,' said the warrior.

'If you did,' said the King of the Bridge, 'you won't ever again kill anybody, after I have finished with you—or else, you're a great warrior.'

They attacked each other, wrestling an arm above and an arm below. They made the hard places soft and the soft places hard; they drew springs of fresh water up through the middle of the grey stones by the dint of hatred and anger and strife. They threw out from themselves four showers of battle: a shower of blood from their waists, a shower of frenzy from their swords, a shower of sweat from their brows and a shower of anger from their teeth. So it went on until the day was drawing to a close and a robin alighted on the warrior's shoulder and said:

'O son of the Irish king, you have come to a bad place to die! It will take me many days to cover your dead body with the leaves of the trees.'

A spasm of anger passed through the warrior. He twisted the King of the Bridge around and sank his body to the waist in the earth; with a second twist, he sank him to the apple of his throat; and with the third twist, he shouted:

'Clay over your body, churl!'

'Let it be so!' said the King of the Bridge. 'But I place you under *geasa* never to halt or rest until you go to the King of the Churchyard and tell him that you have killed the Sow and her Litter and the King of the Bridge.'

The warrior went off and kept travelling until he came to where the King of the Churchyard was. He struck the challenge-pole and didn't leave a calf in a cow, a foal in a mare, a lamb in a ewe, a kid in a she-goat or a piglet in a sow that he didn't turn about nine times in their skins with the sound of the blow! The King of the Churchyard came out to him.

'I killed the Sow and her Litter and the King of the Bridge,' said the warrior.

'You will never again kill anyone, unless you are a better man than I am!' said the King of the Churchyard.

They attacked each other like two mad lions, like two bulls in a field, like two excited rams or two proud enemies that hated each other. They used to throw out from themselves four showers of battle: a shower of blood from their waists, a shower of frenzy from their swords, a shower of sweat from their brows and a shower of anger from their teeth. So it went on until the day was drawing to a close. They didn't know which of them was the better. Then a robin alighted on the warrior's shoulder and said:

'You have come a long way to die here, and it will take me many days to cover your dead body with the leaves of the trees!'

A spasm of anger passed through the warrior's mind, and he pulled himself together. He gave a twist to the King of the Churchyard and sank him to his waist in the earth; with a second twist, he sank him to the apple of his throat, and with the third twist, he shouted:

'That's clay over your body, churl!'

'It is so, best warrior whom I have ever seen.' said the King of the Churchyard. 'But before you cut off my head, I place you under *geasa* never to halt or rest until you go to the Great Cat of the Cave and tell him that you have killed the Sow and her Litter, the King of the Bridge and the King of the Churchyard!'

The warrior went off and kept travelling until he reached the place where the Cat of the Cave had made his cave. He entered the mouth of the cave; it was three miles long from mouth to end. So bright was the light that came from the cat's eyes that the warrior could see a small pin that might have fallen on the floor on the darkest night that ever came, even though the cat was a long distance away from him. He kept walking in through the cave, his sword in his hand, ready for the cat, until he reached the very end where the cat was. He looked around everywhere, and then upwards towards a ledge high up in the cave. He caught sight of a small, little cat, sitting on an arch-way and looking down. From the cat's eyes there shone the brightest and finest light that he had ever seen, and it blinded him when it fell on his own face. He stood in front of the cat and said:

'I have killed the Sow and her Litter, the King of the Bridge and the King of the Churchyard!'

The cat swelled in size until his back reached the roof of the cave. Then he stretched down one of his paws and tore the warrior's body from the waist upwards, and dragged his heart and lungs out on to the floor of the cave. The cat then stretched down his other paw to tear the other side of the warrior's body. As he did so, the warrior caught sight of a black spot under the cat's armpit. He thrust his sword upwards through the spot and pierced his heart. The cat fell down, dead, on to the floor on top of the warrior, who was also dead. So large was the cat's body that it completely covered that of the dead warrior!

That was that! On the following day, the woman and her three brothers went to where the battle used to be fought every day. They found all the enemy lying dead, and so too was the hag who used to bring them back to life. The little pot and the quill lay on the ground beside her. The young woman picked them up and put them in her pocket. They walked on towards where the King of the Bridge lived, as they thought that the warrior might have been killed by him, for they knew that he had always been helping their enemies. They made up their minds to search for the warrior, alive or dead. When they came on the body of the King of the Bridge, they went on to where the King of the Churchyard lived. They found him dead also, and knew that it was the warrior who had killed them all so far. Then they thought that the King of the Churchyard might have sent him to the Great Cat of the Cave, and that he was dead, as the cat had never let anybody escape alive.

They reached the cave of the Great Cat. There was no light within when they entered. They made their way slowly to the end of the cave, and there they found the dead body of the cat. They couldn't see any sign of the warrior, alive or dead. So they turned back again, not knowing where the warrior might be found. The young woman was behind the others and, as she walked along in the dark, her foot struck against the shoe of the warrior, who was lying dead under the cat's body. She shouted to her brothers that he was lying under the body of the cat, and that they should try to release him and bring him back to life with the contents of the pot of the old hag. The four of them tried to lift the cat's body off the warrior, but it was no use—they couldn't even move it. They had to cut the cat's body into pieces with their swords, and lay bare what was underneath it. When they dragged the pieces of the cat aside, they put the heart and lungs back into the warrior's body as they had been when he was alive. When they had that done, they rubbed the contents of the pot to his wounds and to his heart and lungs, and he rose to his feet as well as he had ever been.

There weren't in the whole world three men or a young woman more happy than they, at having found him, and at all their enemies whom they had fought for so long being dead. The warrior and the young woman got married, and they spent seven nights and seven days celebrating. They didn't know whether the first night or the last was the better. Every bite had the taste of honey, and no bite was tasteless!

7 Cū the Smith's Son

THE NAME Cú ('KOO') OF THE hero in this tale signifies Hound. As was the case in the previous story, a number of 'runs' occurs which describe in traditional style the spending of a night in three ways, the hero's sea-voyage, his challenges to successive opponents and his combats with them, and finally the amusing way in which the narrator concludes the tale. The series of quests which the hero has to undertake demand repetition until the final battle with the hag, who in such tales is usually the most formidable opponent, leads towards the happy ending of the tale.

There was a king and queen in Ireland long ago, and they had three sons. One day while the king was out walking, he came upon a very large field, which was covered with trees. He went towards the wood to look at it and saw the most beautiful young woman on whom wind or sun had ever shone. There was a silver fillet on her brow and a golden one around the back of her head. He went up to her. When he was parting from her later on, he said to her:

'I place you under *geasa* to come to this spot nine months from today and to leave here my son or my daughter, although I won't be here myself.'

The King returned home and forgot all about the woman until the last day of the nine months came round. It was a fine summer morning, and he suddenly remembered the conversation he had had with the woman. He went to the place in the wood where he had met her, and found a male child there, fast asleep and covered with sweat. There was nobody else to be seen, so the king lifted the child up in his arms. He was the finest child that had ever been born.

'I'm in a bad fix now,' said the king. 'If the queen finds out that I have a son like this, there will never again be peace between us. But there's a smith who has no children near the palace, and I'll give the child to his wife. I'll ask her to spend a while in bed so that everyone will think that the child is hers.'

That was that! Word went round the country that the smith's wife had a young son. The king and queen were delighted at the news. Everybody came to see the smith's wife and her son, and the name he was given was Cú, the Smith's Son. The child grew to the age of five years, and by that time he was able to confine all the boys in the school in one corner. When he and the king's three sons used to be returning from school every day, Cú used to beat them on the way. The queen said that the smith would have to banish his son lest he would kill her own children.

'Ah!' said the king. 'You must have pity for the smith. All he has is the one son, and you have three.'

The king had great affection for Cú, for he knew that he was his own son. One day when the king was away from home, the queen invited Cú to dinner. He went to the palace, and he and the queen ate their dinner together. When it was over, the queen sat on a chair of gold at the table and pulled out a pack of cards. Cú was sitting on a chair of silver. He won the first game.

'You have won,' said the queen. 'Name your forfeit!'

'I enjoin as a forfeit on you,' said Cú, 'that you allow me to sit on the chair of gold while you sit on the chair of silver.'

She changed her seat to the chair of silver, and Cú sat on the chair of gold. They played another game, and the queen won.

'Name your forfeit!' said Cú, the Smith's Son.

'Soon enough you'll hear it!' said she. 'I put you under injunction and *geasa* to go to Greece and get the king's daughter in marriage. No prince or warrior who has ever gone there to win her hand has returned alive.'

Cú jumped up from the table and went home to the smith's forge, in great anger. He gave a sigh which broke the roof-beam when he entered.

'That's the sigh of a king's son under *geasa*,' said the smith.

'But I'm your son and not the son of a king,' said Cú.

'No,' said the smith. 'You're a king's son. What *geasa* are on you?'

When Cú told him, the smith and his wife started to cry. The king went to the forge when he came home and heard the news. He was heart-broken.

'Son,' said he, 'I'll help you to escape from the *geasa*. The queen told you that you were not to eat a second meal from the same dish or at the same table, drink twice from the same cup or sleep twice in the same bed, until you marry the daughter of the king of Greece. Now, I will give you a golden dish, a golden cup, a golden table and a golden bed every day until you die, and no two of them will be the same.'

''Tis no use, father,' said Cú. 'I must undergo the *geasa*.'

They passed the night, one-third at storytelling, one-third at romancing, and one-third sleeping soundly until next morning. No sooner had day come than Cú got up. He went down to the billowy, wild sea, took a gold ring from his finger and threw it out into the sea. He made a large, capacious ship out of it and hoisted her great, speckled sails, of equal height, length and straightness, to the tops of her masts. He drew in all her mooring ropes and rowed with her sinuous oars, sending the small and the large eels of the eastern and the western seas gliding along the sides of the oars; the rough sand sank to the bottom and the fine sand rose to the top; all providing service and amusement and music for the son of the king of Ireland, until he reached the Eastern World.

He walked up through the kingdom, bearing in his right hand his sword, on which was branded that there wasn't a champion underneath the earth or above it who could overcome him. When he reached the court of the Giant of the Eastern World, he drew his sword and struck the challenge-pole. There wasn't a foal in a mare, a lamb in a ewe, a kid in a she-goat or a child in its mother's womb that he didn't turn around seven times and back again, with the dint of the blow on the pole. The giant's steward came out and asked him what he wanted. Cú answered that he wanted to fight the giant and get the white mare in the stable.

'You won't have long to wait,' said the steward. 'You will have to fight seven score and seven hundred and seventeen hundred great warriors first before you fight the giant.'

Cú looked around him and saw the host of warriors coming at him from every side. He and they attacked one another, and by midday, Cú had slain them all. Next day he struck the challenge-pole again, and the steward came out. He asked Cú what he wanted, and he replied the white mare or a fight with the giant.

'Too soon for you he'll be here!' said the steward. 'The giant is getting ready and he'll be out here to you. Each blow he will strike at you will go from your skin to the flesh, from the flesh to the bone, from the bone to the outer marrow and from that to the inner marrow of your body; and each blow which you will try to strike at him will glance off his body as a drop of rain would from a glass bottle.'

It wasn't long till the huge giant came out. They fought against each other for seven nights and seven days, without either proving better or worse than the other. On the eighth day, they seized each other by the waist. Cú, the Smith's Son, threw the giant and sank him to his two knees in the ground; a second throw sank him to his waist, and a third to his ears.

'Clay on top of you, churl!' said Cú.

'You're the best warrior I have ever met, born of man and woman,' said the giant. 'Release me, and I'll let you have half of my kingdom while I live and all of it after my death; and myself and the white mare will serve you wherever you go in the world.'

'Bad scran to you!' said Cú. 'Many's the place where I could get the fill of my belly of food and you wouldn't. Still, it won't do me any good to kill you.'

Cú took hold of the giant's two ears and, in pulling him up out of the ground, made them seven yards long. They went into the giant's court and ate and drank. They vied with each other in feats of valour and magic, but for each gift the giant had, Cú had seven. Then they slept until morning. Cú arose at daybreak and asked the giant where was the white mare.

'Take this bridle,' said the giant, 'and shake it at the gap of the first field you come to. Take away the first horse that comes out and puts her head into the bridle.'

Cú went out, with the bridle in his hand, till he reached the field. He shook the bridle, and it was the worst-looking horse in the field that came and put her head into the bridle. Cú hated her appearance.

'I won't have you long in my company,' said Cú. 'I'll drown you in the first hole I come to.'

He pulled the poor horse after him by the bridle, and when he was passing a quagmire, he was on the point of shouldering the horse into it to drown her, when the horse spoke.

'Shame on you!' said the horse. 'If you were the son of a king and queen, you would cut a sapling and jump on my back; you'd then strike me on the upper rib with it, and if I won't be able to give you a good ride, day won't dawn tomorrow.'

Cú cut a sapling and jumped on the horse's back. He struck her on the upper rib, and she rose into the air. She performed three feats of agility and prowess underneath the sun, and never stopped or stayed till she brought him to the front of the palace of the King of Greece.

'Get down off my back now!' said the horse. 'This is the court of the King of Greece, and he has the most beautiful daughter that has been heard of in the world. Princes and warriors from everywhere are coming to get her, but none of them gets her or will. Her father has high hopes that a son of a king and queen in Ireland will come for her; he is interested only in suitors from Ireland and wants one of them to be his son-in-law. The king's garden and farm are the finest in the world, with trees and fruit and pathways. Now, when you get up on my back, face me towards the gate and make me trample on all the fine things in the garden. They will say that only a son of a king and queen would do that, taking no notice of the fine things there, being accustomed to finer things at home. And when you put me up for the night, don't put me into the same stable as the king's black mare.'

Cú jumped up on the horse's back again and faced her towards the gate. She passed over it and started to frisk through the garden, destroying all that was in it. When she reached the door of the court, the king's daughter was upstairs, looking out at the warrior. She ran down to her father with the news that no warrior as fine had ever before come to Greece, nor would he come again. She fell in love with Cú the moment she saw him. She went with her father to the door to welcome the warrior, and all shook hands. They then sat down together and spent the time until supper was ready. When supper was over, Cú told the king that he was under *geasa* to get his daughter in marriage. The king asked him his name and where he came from.

'I'm the son of a king and queen in Ireland,' said he. 'The name they call me by is Cú, the Smith's Son.'

'As a husband for my daughter, there's no man under the sun or in any kingdom whom I'd prefer to the son of a king and queen in Ireland. If you're a king's son, I'll give her to you after twenty-one days. My daughter and I will go to Ireland to find out about you, and if you are what you say, I'll give you my daughter.'

They spent that night, one-third storytelling, one-third romancing, and one-third sleeping soundly till next morning.

No sooner had day dawned than Cú got up. He shook hands with the King of Greece and his daughter and went out to the stable where the white mare was. When he jumped on her back, she leaped over the court, performed three feats of agility and prowess underneath the sun and never stopped until she came down in a field near the palace of the King of Ireland. The horse then spoke and asked Cú to dismount. He did so, and when he pulled off the bridle, she went to take a drink from a well. She sank down into the well and was lost to sight. Cú went indoors to his father, and there wasn't a happier man than the king to be found when he saw his son.

Cú told his father that the King of Greece and his daughter would arrive in twenty-one days' time, and that he would marry her when they came. The king was delighted. He ordered a silver road to be made from the quay to the palace in preparation for the King of Greece and his daughter. The road was finished and everything was ready in time, but when the twenty-one days were up, the king and his daughter had not arrived. Nor did they come during the next twenty-one days. Cú was heartbroken; he didn't know what had prevented the king and his daughter from coming. One day, filled with sorrow, he went out for a walk and reached the field where the white mare had sunk down into the well. She rose out of the well, and when he went up to her, she spoke. Many things had happened to the King of Greece, she said: a great warrior had arrived from the Western World and taken off his daughter, who had placed *geasa* on the warrior not to know whether she was woman or man until the end of a year and a day.

'The king tried to prevent his daughter from being taken away, but in the struggle, the king, though a fine warrior himself, had lost two of his front teeth. Since then, he has become like an old, grey-haired man. If he got the teeth back again, he would be as strong and youthful as he had been before. Get up on my back!' said the horse.

When he did so, she leaped upwards and performed three feats of agility and prowess underneath the sun; then she went ahead and never stopped until she reached Greece.

'Put me into the stable with the king's horse,' said she. 'Then go into the palace and when you meet the king, he will tell you more about what has happened than I can, if you intend to go to look for his daughter in the Western World.'

When he entered the palace, he found the king an old, grey-haired man, stricken in body and dull of mind, because of the abuse he had received and the loss of his daughter. When Cú spoke to him the old king gave him a thousand and a hundred welcomes and kissed him. Then the tears ran down his cheeks as he told Cú what had happened two days before they were to go to Ireland, when a great warrior had come from the Western World and taken off his daughter. The name of the warrior was Ard-Mhac-Léinn, he said.

'I place myself under *geasa*,' said Cú, 'not to sleep twice in the same bed or spend a second night in the same house or drink a second time from any cup until I go to Ard-Mhac-Léinn in the Western World, and either lose my head or cut off his, because of the young princess.'

They passed the night, one-third at storytelling, one-third at romancing, and one-third in sound sleep until the following morning. Cú got up as soon as day broke. He rubbed his palms to his two eyes, to his sides and to his limbs. He said his prayers, combed his hair and asked God to direct him. He bade goodbye to the King of Greece and set out. He sailed away in his ship at double speed for seven nights and seven days, ploughing the eastern and the western seas, which had never been ploughed before nor will again. The small eels and the big eels leaped on board coiled together, making service, sport and music for the son of the King of Ireland on his way to the Western World. When he reached the harbour there, he turned his ship into a grey stone on the shore, covered with seaweed, safe from wind and sun.

He walked up through the kingdom, and a fine kingdom it was. He struck the challenge-pole, and there wasn't a place in the kingdom where the sound of the blow wasn't heard. The steward came out and asked him what he wanted. Cú said that he wanted to fight the warrior and rescue the king's daughter.

'You won't be kept long waiting,' said the steward. 'The greatest warrior in the world is getting ready and putting on his armour. He'll be here within a quarter of an hour.'

Ard-Mhac Léinn soon came out and the two attacked each other. They fought on the ground with two swords, making the soft places hard and the hard places soft, the high places low and the low places high, and drawing wells of fresh water up through the stones by dint of fighting and hard combat. They spent part of seven nights and seven days without either of them overcoming the other. Then they ran towards each other and grappled at the waist. The Son of the King of Ireland knocked down the warrior and cut off his head for all the kingdom to see.

He went into the court to the young princess. She smothered him with tears and dried him with kisses, with smooth silken towels and with the hair of her own head. Then they went down to the shore. He turned the stone back into a ship, raised his large, billowing sails, and they sailed home to Greece. He was married immediately to the daughter of the King of Greece, and they were the finest pair that sun ever shone on.

Another warrior called Mac Mhaol, a huge giant, had taken the king's two teeth away from Ard-Mhac-Léinn, so Cú placed himself under *geasa* to recover them or die in the attempt. He jumped on the back of his horse and never stopped till he arrived at the court of Mac Mhaol. He struck the challenge-pole and the steward came out and asked him what he wanted.

'I want the two teeth of the king of Greece,' said Cú, 'and if I don't get them, I'll fight Mac Mhaol, hand to hand.'

'Too soon he'll come to you!' said the steward. 'He'll be with you soon.'

The giant came out. Cú knocked him down before three-quarters of an hour were past. When Cú had sunk him to his neck in the ground, Mac Mhaol asked for pardon and mercy, and if his life were spared, he would go through the world as a servant of Cú.

'I'm not looking for either a servant boy or girl,' said Cú. 'All I want is the two front teeth of the King of Greece.'

'I'd gladly give them to you,' said Mac Mhaol, 'but another giant has taken them from me.'

'Will you come with me to that giant's house?' asked Cú.

'I won't,' said Mac Mhaol, 'because of the pains and punishment I suffered from him when he took away the teeth of the King of Greece from me. I would advise you not to go near him, for there has never been born in this world, nor will there be born again, any man or warrior who can stand against the big giant.'

The Son of the King of Ireland, in anger, gave up pleading with him, and, sword in hand, he jumped up on his horse. Within three quarters of an hour, he was at the court of the great giant. When he struck the challenge-pole, the steward came out and asked what he wanted. Cú, the Smith's Son, said that he wanted the two front teeth of the King of Greece or else a fight with the big giant.

'Too soon he'll come to you!' said the steward. 'The big giant is getting ready, and he'll be out to you soon.'

It wasn't long till the big giant came out. They attacked each other as would two fiery dragons or two hawks, and fought for seven nights and seven days. Neither of them could overcome the other. Then they grappled each other around the waist, made the soft ground hard and the hard ground soft, the low places high and the high places low, drew wells of fresh water up through the stone flags and choked and exhausted each other with the dint of fighting and hard combat. Then the Son of the King of Ireland knocked him down; with one throw he sank the giant to his two knees into the ground, with a second he sank him to his buttocks and with a third to his neck.

'Clay over your head, warrior!' said Cú, the Smith's Son.

'You have won, Son of the King of Ireland!' said the big giant. 'Let me free and I'll give you half of my kingdom during my life and all of it after my death. And I'll be your servant, if you spare my life.'

'I'm not looking for a servant boy or girl,' said Cú. 'All I want is the two front teeth of the King of Greece.'

'That's something I can't give you,' said the big giant. 'A hag who has killed hundreds took them from me three months ago.'

'Show me where her kingdom is,' said the Son of the King of Ireland.

'I won't,' said the big giant. 'She made me suffer so much, that I never want to see her again in this world. And I want to tell you that even if you were seven hundred times as good a warrior as you are, the hag would kill you in a quarter of an hour.'

'Show me where her kingdom is,' said the Son of the King of Ireland.

'I'll do that,' said the giant. 'There's a river flowing down between here and there, and you must fill three bottles with water from the river. There's a magic fog over her kingdom, because of the hag's devilish magic, and from the moment you take a step on her land, the fog will be in front of you and behind and all around you, so that you can't see anything. But when you sprinkle a drop of the water ahead of you, the fog will disperse for that length, but it will close in behind you. You can sprinkle the water until the three bottles are empty, but if you haven't caught sight of the hag's court by then, you are lost!'

The giant pointed the way to the hag's court, and Cú set out until he reached it. He filled the three bottles of water and started to sprinkle it ahead of him. The fog in front disappeared as he sprinkled the water in front, but it closed in behind until he had used up two bottles. He took the third bottle, and when he had sprinkled the last drops from it, he caught sight of the hag's court. He walked straight up to the challenge-pole and struck it. He didn't leave a foal in a mare, a lamb in a ewe, a kid in a she-goat or a child in its mother's womb that he didn't turn around nine times and back again. The big hag came out, her sword in her right hand and the hem of her coat in her mouth. In fury, she faced the Son of the King of Ireland. They attacked each other with their two swords, and the hag spent until midday mocking and deriding him, as she sliced off his flesh. She dragged him down to the ground and gave him every kind of abuse. When Cú saw his sorry state and that he had not long to live, he ran backwards from her, and then rushed forward and struck her in the forehead with his sword. His sword broke in two at the hilt, and did not injure the hag. He asked the hag for time to recover his sword again. This she granted before she went back to her court. The Son of the King of Ireland looked around him; he was a stranger to the kingdom and was in great pain. A quarter of a mile away, he saw a young woman wringing her hands and wailing.

'I have always heard in Ireland,' said he, 'that it wasn't right to pass by a wailing woman without asking her what was her trouble.'

He went towards her house and stood at the closed door. He could hear her telling her father, who was in bed, that his daughter's son from Ireland was being killed today by the big hag, and that he was almost dead.

'May God help us!' cried the old man. 'Many was the day when the big hag wouldn't stand long against myself! Even today, I'd defeat her only for being overcome by her magic, so that I can't get out of this bed as long as she's alive.'

When the Son of the King of Ireland heard this talk between the young woman and her father, he knew that the old man's daughter was his own mother. That was good and it wasn't bad! He went into the house.

'I welcome you and salute you,' said the old man. 'You are the son of my daughter from Ireland. Isn't it to a bad place you have come to die today, like myself, at the hands of the big hag!'

The old man's daughter, Cú's aunt, went over to him, and it looked as if she would never stop crying.

'Give me your hand, son, till I see are you strong,' said the old man.

Cú went over to him and held out his hand. The old man took hold of it and squeezed it so hard that the blood oozed out through the tips of four fingers.

'You're still young, son,' said he, 'and you're not strong enough for the big hag. There's a big flag-stone outside there, and my sword is underneath it. It has twice as much magical power as the hag's sword has. If you are able to raise up the flag-stone even at the third attempt, I'll have a good opinion of you; but if you don't, it means your death and mine, and she won't leave a person or an animal alive in Ireland.'

Cú rushed out immediately and tried to raise the stone, but failed to move it. He failed also the second time. He tried a third time, with all his strength and fury, and turned the under-side up and the top-side down. He seized the sword and swung it so that its tip touched its hilt. No sooner had he done that than the big hag stood before him. The pair of them attacked each other for seven nights and seven days, without either proving better or worse than the other. Neither of them could win the upperhand. They made soft places hard and hard places soft, low places high and high places low. Then they seized each other by the neck. With one twist, Cú buried the big hag to her knees, with a second to her waist, and with a third to the lobes of her two ears.

'Clay over you, hag!' said Cú.

'Yes,' said she, 'you are the best warrior born of man and

woman that I have ever met. Let me go, and I'll give you half of my kingdom during my life and the whole of it after my death, and I'll be your servant wherever you go in the world.'

'I want nothing in the world from you but the two front teeth of the King of Greece,' said Cú.

'I'll give them to you, if you let me go,' said the hag.

'I won't let you go till I get them first,' said Cú.

She gave keys to a servant boy that she had to open the room where the teeth were in a box. The boy quickly came back with the teeth. He handed them to Cú, the Smith's Son, and when he got them, he took his sword in his right hand.

'On what will I test the edge of my sword?' said he to the hag.

'Try it on the stump of that ugly old tree over there,' said she.

'I don't see anything uglier than your own head,' said he.

He drew his sword on her neck and cut off her head. The head was whistling as it went up into the air and humming as it fell down, in an endeavour to attach itself to the body again. But Cú made no mistake. He kicked the skull with his right foot and drove it over six ridges and six acres off.

' 'Twas well for you that you did that!' said the head. 'If I joined up with the body again, half of the Fianna wouldn't be able to sever me again.'

'It wasn't to let you back again that I cut you off in the first place, you wretch!' said Cú.

At that moment, the fog disappeared from the kingdom, and the evil curse ceased to have power. Cú's aunt ran in to her father and told him that the Son of the King of Ireland had killed the big hag. The old man didn't believe her, for he thought that there wasn't a warrior under the sun who could cut off her head. Then Cú went in and told him that the big hag was dead.

'I find it hard to believe, son,' said the old man, 'for I was sure that a man or woman able to fight the big hag would never be born.'

The old man stood at the door and saw that the evil fog of the hag had lifted from the kingdom, and he became as fine a warrior as Cú immediately. They spent a joyful night. Cú set out next morning and reached Greece within three weeks. When he gave his two front teeth to the king, he too became a fine young warrior again. Cú spent a week there with his wife and her father. Then one day when he was out of doors, he remembered his own father and was sad that he hadn't seen him for a long time. He made up his mind on the spot to set out for Ireland to see him. He pulled out his horse and told her that he was going on a visit to his father in Ireland. The horse ordered him to get on her back and when he did so, she did three kinds of feats and valour underneath the sun for him, before she landed him in the same field near the palace of the King of Ireland.

'Get off my back now,' said the horse, and she let a ring of gold fall from her mouth. 'When you go into your father's palace, nobody there will pretend to have greater welcome for you than your stepmother, although nobody hates you more. She will ask you have you brought her any present. Tell her that you have, that you weren't going to forget her. "What is it?" she'll ask you. "A gold ring", you'll tell her. "Give it to me till I put it on my finger," she'll say. She'll stretch out her hand, and you'll put the ring on her finger. Tell her to squeeze the ring, and when she does, she'll start to scream, as it will hurt her very much. Ask her, in the presence of the king, who was father to her eldest son. She will say that he was the king. You'll say he wasn't, and order her to squeeze the ring more tightly. When she does that, ask her again who was father to her eldest son, and she will admit he was the man who looked after the king's calves. "Who was father to your second son?" you will ask her. "The kitchen scullion," she will say. Ask her then who was father to her third son and she will say he was the swineherd.'

Cú did what the horse had told him, and the ring made the stepmother tell the whole truth.

'What she is saying is the truth,' said the king. 'Her three sons are nothing to me; if they were mine, they'd be better men than they are. 'Tis you who are my son,' said he to Cú; 'I know that well, and since that is so, the kingdom will be yours when I die.'

The king was seized with great anger. He sent twenty-one men for three nights and three days with carts to draw turf for a bonfire. He got twelve barrels of tar and sprinkled the turf with it, before setting the whole lot afire. The flames rose half-way up to the sky. He then took hold of the queen and her three sons and threw them into the fire so that they were burned to the bone. When Cú entered the palace, his father was filled with pride at being with him again. They sat down and stayed until morning talking about all that had happened.

After breakfast, they went out for a walk, and came to the field where the white mare used to land. They walked towards the well into which the mare used to sink out of sight. The king glanced around and saw the most beautiful woman the sun had ever shone upon rising up out of the well.

'Look around, son, and see your mother,' said the king.

Cú and the king rushed towards her and began to kiss and embrace her. It looked as if Cú would never let her go. Then the king married her, and they had a wedding-feast that lasted for seven nights and seven days. When it was over, Cú said that he should go back to his own wife. The three of them set out for Greece, where they spent seven more nights and days feasting and celebrating. After spending a year there, Cú and his wife went to Ireland.

That's my story, true and false! Long life to the company who have listened to it and to the man who has told it! The dear blessing of God and of the Church on the souls of the dead, amen! All I got was stockings of thick butter-milk and shoes of paper! I threw them back. Those who gave them to me were drowned, but I came safe! And devil a word of news of them has Éamonn a Búrc (the storyteller himself) got from them for the past six months!

II Ordinary Folktales

8 Judas

THIS APOCRYPHAL LEGEND OF Judas Iscariot, the betrayer of Jesus Christ, is, in the following version a curious blend of the classical tale about Oedipus, king of Thebes, who killed his father and married his own mother (Judas takes the part of Oedipus in this version) and of the story of the betrayal as found in the New Testament. The present oral version has borrowed heavily from both sources. For the final episode which tells of Judas' sufferings in hell and of his temporary respite to cool himself, see the reference to the Life of Saint Brendan, in The Lives of the Irish

Saints, mentioned in the Notes. That part of the legend is medieval, though the motif may be much older.

There was a poor scholar travelling around long, long ago. He came to a house where a baby, a son, had just been born. The poor scholar told the child's mother and the people of the house that there was a dire fate in store for the new child; that he would pass through many hardships and would do much harm when he reached manhood. He said that the child, when a man, would kill his own father, would marry his mother and would be involved in the Crucifixion of the Saviour.

The child was baptised, anyway, and was given the name Judas. During the baptism, it was noticed that he had a black cross marked on his back, between his two shoulder-blades.

His mother could not put out of her mind what the poor scholar had said; it was causing her much anxiety. She finally grew to be afraid of her son, and made up her mind to get rid of him. She got a box ready for him, put him into it, with some food and milk, and set it afloat on a river or on the sea which was close by. The box drifted on the current before the wind until it reached a distant country. There was a man walking by the shore and he found the box, with the child inside. He took the child to the house of a gentleman, and when the gentleman saw him, he decided to keep him and rear him with his own sons.

Things went on like that for some years until Judas had grown up to be a young fellow, at the edge of manhood. One day he was playing ball with the gentleman's sons, and he struck one of them with a stick and broke his leg accidentally. This caused great uproar, and Judas was told that he had been found cast up on the shore, and that no one knew who he was or to whom he belonged. Until then Judas had thought that he was one of the gentleman's sons. On finding out that he wasn't, he left the place and travelled before him till he came to a house in which a young married couple was living. He told the man of the house that he was looking for work as a servant-boy. The man said that he needed a workman, so they made a bargain between them. Judas spent seven years there, and nothing unusual happened to him.

The man of the house had an orchard, and people used to come by night to steal the apples. One night Judas was set to watch the orchard. He climbed a tree, taking an armful of stones with him. Sometime out in the night, a man entered the orchard; he stood under the tree on which Judas was and started to shake the branches to make the apples fall down. Judas let a stone fall on him and hit him on the top of his head. The man was killed. Judas did not know who the man was and he didn't wait to find out either. Next day he left the district before he would be arrested for killing the man.

He travelled on, not knowing where he was going, until he reached a place a long distance from where the killing had taken place. There he got work from a farmer. He spent a number of years there and got on fairly well. The farmer was very friendly with him and, to make things better for him, started to encourage him to marry a widow who lived nearby. He mentioned this so often that Judas said at last that he would agree to marry her, if she was willing. One night Judas and the farmer went to the widow; the match was made, and the pair got married before very long.

That was all right until one day, when Judas was changing some wet clothes that he was wearing, his wife noticed the black cross between his two-shoulder-blades. The life nearly left her, with the fright when she saw it, for she knew immediately that her son was her husband. Judas knew nothing until she told him about his birth and the prophecy of the poor scholar and everything. During the conversation, he also learned that it was his own father he had killed with the stone in the orchard. So all that the poor scholar had said had come true so far.

Judas then set out on his travels again, sad and heart-broken and full of shame on account of all the harm he had done, until he came to the place where Our Saviour was going about, teaching the people. He followed Jesus from place to place and at last was taken on as one of the disciples. He was all right for a while, very sorry for all that he had done, but by degrees avarice and miserliness increased in his heart. He found fault with Mary Magdalen for rubbing a box of ointment on the Saviour's feet, saying that the money that bought it should have been given to the poor. At last, he went to the bad so far as to make up his mind to betray Jesus for money. Having done so, he went to the Last Supper with the other disciples. When Our Lord said that one of the disciples was going to betray Him, Judas asked, as well as the others, 'Is it I, Lord?' Jesus told the others secretly that Judas was the traitor. Soon afterwards, Judas left the room. Regret came over him for what he had done, and he went to the leaders who had given him the money for the betrayal and threw it back to them, saying that he had acted wrongly. Little satisfaction he got from them, and they used the money to buy a burial-place for strangers. Judas left them and, full of sorrow and regret and heart-break, he went and hanged himself with a rope from a tree.

Many years later, there were monks sailing the seas, fishing to the west of Brandon. They saw what looked liked a little island rising out of the sea. They went towards it, and when they came near, they saw that it was an island of ice on which a man was walking. They went near enough to speak to him and asked who he was or what had caused him to be in such a place. He told them that he was Judas. 'I am Judas who betrayed Christ, and I'm damned for ever in Hell, except for one day each year like this when I'm allowed to come here to cool myself. I have been here since sunrise today, but when the sun sets in the evening, a crowd of devils will come from Hell to take me with them again. If ye pray earnestly for me, I may get a second day each year to come here.'

The monks had such great pity for him that they started to pray to God that He would grant a second day's space. By then, the sun was about to set, and the monks saw a crowd of devils coming through the sea, like whales. They weren't able to land on the island of ice, however, for Judas had been granted the following day also through the prayers of the monks. When the monks saw this, they hoisted sail and made for home.

9 *The Best Way to God*

THIS TALE IS WELL-KNOWN in Ireland. It tells of visions of life beyond the grave which lies in store for three men: a schoolmaster, a farmer and a priest. At the same time, it resembles a story of the *exempla* (moral sermon-tales) type, in that it points to the best way of life here on earth. As the person who seems to have chosen the surest livelihood leading to God is the farmer, one is tempted to hazard an opinion that the story was composed by a member of that class!

A farmer was returning home from town one evening. It was fairly late. He had a horse and cart and on the way he met a priest walking along. At that time priests and gentlemen hadn't motor-cars like they have now. The farmer spoke to the priest.

'Would you like to sit into the front of the cart?' he asked. 'I have a fine, strong horse, and I'll give you a lift for a part of the road.'

'Thank you!' said the priest. ''Tis a friend that would do that!'

He sat into the cart, and they started to chat. They hadn't gone far when a strapping schoolmaster met them.

'Come into the cart, my man!' said the farmer. 'This is a long road, and we'll be company to each other.'

The schoolmaster sat in, and the three of them talked, while the horse shortened the road at a good pace. An argument arose between them, each of them praising his own way of life. The priest said that his own calling was the best. The schoolmaster boasted that it was he who taught the priests, doctors, students and scholars their religion and learning and how to read and write.

'I'd say that my way is better than either of yours,' said the farmer. 'Isn't it my hard work and my land that's feeding each of you and the doctors as well?'

They went on arguing and getting angry with one another, until whom should they met at a crossroads but a well-dressed stranger.

'God and Mary to you!' said the farmer.

'God and Mary and Patrick to you!' said the stranger.

''Tis someone like you we wanted to meet,' said the farmer. 'We have been arguing along the road about certain things, but we grew so tired of it that we said we'd let the first man we met decide which of us was right.'

'Very well,' said the stranger.

The farmer told him what the argument was about.

'I won't be able to decide between ye until sunrise tomorrow morning,' said the stranger. 'Ye must go up on that round hill over there and spend the night there. In the morning each of you can tell me what he has seen, and then I'll be able to decide who is right.'

'I'd gladly go on the hill,' said the farmer, 'but who will mind my horse?'

'My hand and my word to you,' said the stranger, 'that your

horse will be safe and sound before you in the morning.'

'All right,' said the farmer.

The three of them went up the hill and, whatever magic came over them, they lost sight of one another. Each of them went his own way.

The schoolmaster came to a garden. He entered, and his eye had never before seen a finer place. There wasn't a flower or a fruit that wasn't growing there, and so sweet was the perfume of the flowers that he didn't feel hungry. All he wished for was to be walking through the flowers! He thought that he should bring back some tokens to the stranger, so he picked some of the apples and pears and filled his pockets with them.

'There's no doubt that I'll have something to show in the morning!' said he.

The place the priest came to was a deep, lonely glen, with a smooth, even surface. In the centre of it was what seemed to be a hay-cock, and a great many people, small and tall, and some of them old, playing with a hard, hempen ball. Whenever one of the men caught the ball, he would run and strike the hay-cock a hard blow with it. The ball would rebound and roll down the slope. Then another man would catch it and do the same. The priest spent the whole night watching them and wondering what they were at.

As for the farmer, he came upon a fine-looking house on the hill. The door was open, and he went in. There was a fine fire burning inside and the house was well-lighted. He couldn't see anybody, so he pulled a chair towards the fire. When he glanced over his right shoulder, he saw a table in the centre of the floor, laden with all kinds of food.

'I may as well eat the food, at any rate,' said he. 'There's nobody to interfere with me, and why should I be hungry, with food on the table?'

He pulled his chair to the table and ate and drank his fill. After the meal, it wasn't long until he felt like lying down. He glanced towards the lower part of the house and saw two well-dressed beds there. He decided to go to sleep in one of them. He took off his clothes and got into one of the beds, and just as a drowsy sleep was coming over him, didn't the bed give a jump and throw him out on to the floor!

'I must have had a dream or a nightmare and fallen out of the bed!' said he.

He got up and went into the bed again.

'I'll try you a second time, at any rate!' said he.

No sooner had he got into the bed than it gave a turn and threw him on to the floor.

'I won't have to be depending on you,' said he to the bed, 'while there's a bed as good as you at the other side that might let me sleep in it.'

He turned towards the second bed and got into it. No sooner had he lain down than he fell into a deep sleep, and he didn't awaken until day was dawning. What roused him was the singing of birds, and when he opened his eyes, the clear, blue morning sky was above him, and the birds were singing merrily. When he turned his head, he rubbed his eyes to take the sleep off them.

'Lord of miracles!' he cried. 'Where has the house where I spent last night gone to? If anyone saw me like this, with no stitch of clothes on me, they'd say I was a fool!'

He put on his clothes and went down the side of the hill. The priest and the schoolmaster joined him, and they made their way together to the crossroads. The stranger was there before them, taking care of the farmer's horse.

'Well, here ye are!' said the stranger.

'We are,' said the farmer.

'Tell me now,' said the stranger to the priest, 'what wonders have you seen during the night?'

The priest told him about the glen where he had seen the men throwing a ball against a hay-cock.

'You yourself are that hay-cock,' said the stranger. 'The young children who were throwing the ball at you are those you let die without baptism, the old are the people you let die without anointing, and the young men are those whom you neglected to instruct from their youth onwards. You had better look out,' said the stranger. 'If you don't do penance and carry out your duties better than you are doing, you'll pay for it!'

The poor priest trembled in hand and foot, and no wonder.

'What did you see last night?' said the stranger to the schoolmaster.

'I saw a most wonderful garden, sir,' said the schoolmaster, 'the finest anybody had ever walked through. I spent the night going through it, and I wouldn't ask for food or drink as long as I could do that. The fruit and the flowers were so beautiful and so sweet-smelling, that I was ready to faint. There were all kinds of fruit there, and I brought some of them with me to show to you.'

'Show them to me,' said the stranger.

The schoolmaster put his hand into his pockets, but after all his searching, all he could find was a single apple.

'God bless my soul!' said he. 'I have only one apple! Where did the others go?'

'That's just like the way you have spent your life,' said the stranger. 'The only alms you have ever given away is one shilling that you gave to a poor woman, who had two children, and that apple stands for that shilling. Change your ways! Be careful, and be more kind to the poor and give alms!'

'What did you see?' he asked the farmer.

The farmer told him about the fine house he had come to, about the meal he had eaten and about the two beds, and about the birds that roused him with their singing in the morning.

'The first bed you went into,' said the stranger, 'threw you out again, because it is the bed that has been prepared for you in Heaven, and you cannot sleep in it until after your death. The other comfortable bed in which you slept soundly is the good bed, which you and your father before you, have always ready for poor travellers. You have never let a poor person go away hungry from your house. Keep on like you have been doing! You have a better way to God than either of these two. Goodbye now,' said he to the three of them, ' and may the blessing of God go with you on the road!'

The three of them went their own ways, and as good as the farmer's life was up to that time, it was still better for the rest of his life.

10 The King of Sunday

THIS CURIOUS TALE HAS A VERY strong medieval flavour. Its theme is a universal one: the attempt by the Devil to take a human being into his power. Here, however, is a strong hint of divine intervention, through the medium of Saint Joseph, to thwart the evil intention. The journey to the otherworld through the cold sea of Death, to the island of cleansing fire and healing grace (Purgatory, perhaps), passing the fat and lean kine of the Old Testament story, and finally witnessing the Saviour shedding his blood again during the Mass, are a strange blend of popular Catholic belief and Biblical tradition.

There was a man there long ago, and he was known as the King of Sunday, he was so pious. He was fairly well-off and wanted for nothing. He had a son and a daughter, and she was more beautiful and pleasing than any other woman in the world.

When she was twenty years of age, her father sent word around the country that he would give her in marriage to whichever man could sow a hundred-weight of oats, get it to grow, reap it, thresh it, sell the grain and bring the price of it home to him—all to be done in the one day! He also said that any man who tried to do the work and failed would lose his head.

There was a fine spade-man in the kingdom and he told his neighbours that he would try to do all the king asked in one day in order to win his daughter. The poor fellow went to the King of Sunday and asked him to get a hundred-weight of oats for him and show him where he was to plant the grain. The king gave him the oats and showed him the place, and the man was putting the bones out through his skin with the dint of hard work till he had all the seed planted. He was as badly off as ever then, for he couldn't get the crop to grow the same day. Still, the king didn't put him to death, although that was in the bargain, as he was only a poor man who was working hard to try to make a living; the king also saw that he was a simple man, or he wouldn't have attempted such a hard task to be done all in the one day.

One Sunday morning, another man arrived at the king's palace and said that he would do all the work in one day. 'Very well,' said the king; 'you had better start now.'

'I won't start until tomorrow morning,' replied the man, 'for I want to avoid Sunday.'

No sooner had he left than another man arrived, riding a white horse, whose legs were bound in straw-ropes up to the knees; the rider himself was dressed in strange-looking clothes. 'There's no use in trying,' said the king. 'How do you know what I want?' asked the rider. 'I'd say you're going to try to carry out this task of mine,' replied the king. 'I can't deny that that is why I'm here,' said the man. 'You're late,' said the king; 'a man has just been here and gone and he said he'd do it tomorrow.' 'If you take my advice,' said the rider, ' you'll let me try to do it today; that other fellow may not come back any more, and you'll be as badly off as ever.' 'Very well,' said the king; 'do the work and, if you complete it, my daughter might get a worse husband than you.'

The man of the white horse got the hundred-weight of oats, he sprinkled the seeds on the ground and planted them; they grew up immediately; he reaped the crop, threshed it, and sold the grain all in the one day. The king couldn't believe his eyes when he was handed the money in the evening. He gave the rider his daughter, with his blessing, and the girl didn't object as she decided that her new husband had power from God. He brought out his white horse, with straw-ropes around its legs to its knees, put the girl on its back in front of himself, and he, dressed in his strange clothes, holding the reins behind her. They travelled on ever and ever until they reached wherever they were bound for.

When they were gone a year, the king's son said that it was time they had some news or account from his sister, and if they didn't get any before the week was out, he himself would set out to find her. The week passed without any news coming, any more than during the year since they had left. The son then said that he would wait no longer.

He got ready his horse and prepared himself for the road. He was able to take a good supply of food and drink with him, and his pockets weren't short of money either. He kept going all day till night came on him and he reached a house in which he found an old woman, spent with age. Her forehead was wrinkled and her eyes were closed through age. He stayed in that house until next morning and when he was setting out again he asked the old woman had she any account of a young woman who was travelling in the company of a man, who had a white horse whose legs were bound with straw-ropes.

'I saw a woman like that passing this way a year ago today,' said the old woman, 'and if she kept on travelling since then, she'd be far off now.'

He left goodbye and his blessing with the old woman and rode as fast as he could along the road which he thought his sister and the man of the white horse had followed. He kept going as he had done the day before and when the night came he had to stop. He asked about where he might get lodgings and was directed to a lonely house where an old man lived by himself. He got plenty to eat and drink from the old man and he stayed the night there, though they didn't sleep a wink, only talking and discoursing till the morning. He asked the old man had he seen a young woman passing by on a white horse, with straw-ropes on its legs; he said that he had seen such a girl riding on a white horse in front of a man who was holding the reins—they had passed by his door and, if they had kept on riding since, they would be far away by now. The brother set off again next morning on his horse and he followed the road which the old man pointed out to him.

He wasn't long travelling that day when he saw a fine big house in a wood, and there was a beautiful, young woman looking out through the stair-window. He rode towards the house, and when he came near it the woman wasn't at the window any longer. She was standing at the door to welcome him. She shook him by the hand and kissed him when he reached her. She was his sister. He asked her how she liked the place and had she heavy work to do.

'I like the place well,' she said, ' and all I have to do is to wash towels and iron them.'

The man who had taken his sister away came in and he had a hundred welcomes for him like she had. The man told him to stay a few days, and that his sister would be returning home with him to the joy of her father. They all went to sleep when bed-time came. At dawn the man of the house got up and spent an hour on his knees thanking God. He laid out work for the son of the King of Sunday: to drive out three cows to pasture, to follow them wherever they went and to bring home samples of whatever food and drink they would take during the day.

He drove out the cows in the morning, and they faced towards the sea. They plunged into it and he did the same, holding on to the tail of the last cow, and they swam out until they reached an island in the very middle of the sea. The cows went ashore on the island and he followed them. They passed through a huge, terrible wall of fire, and were burned to the bone. He followed them through the fire and was also burned. The cows went to a well at the other side of the fire and when they drank from it, they were as well as they had been before. He bent down and drank from the well also and was healed. He then took a drop of the well-water and placed it in a bottle, as he has been ordered to do.

The cows then turned aside and he followed them. He saw a man, whose nose was dirty, tied to a gate. The man asked him to clean his nose, but was refused, through conceit. However, after a while, the son of the King of Sunday grew sorry for his refusal, so he returned and cleaned the man's nose. No sooner had he done so than the man was released from the gate and he started to dance in the middle of the road.

He followed the cows along and saw a field in which rich grass was growing. However, the cattle which were in the field were so thin that their bones were sticking out through their skins with the dint of hunger. Nearby was a second field, bare as the hearthstone, but the cattle in it were shaking with fat. He was greatly surprised by these sights.

He followed the cows along until some of them went into a large field from him. Each cow ate a piece of an apple, leaving some behind, which he put into a bag that he had. He then heard a bell ringing, and the thought struck him that Mass might be about to begin. When the cows heard the bell, they lay down on the road, and he went in to the church to Mass. When he was inside, he saw a priest on the altar and a clerk attending him. At each word which the priest uttered, a sweat of blood came through his body, and the clerk wiped away the blood with towels. He remained there until Mass was over. When the priest came down from the altar, the congregation left the church and he along with them. The cows, which had been lying down, stood up and never stopped till he followed them home again.

He had a long story to tell his sister when they met, and he had it only half-told when the man of the house arrived home, carrying towels, dripping blood, under his oxter. He asked the son of the King of Sunday had he any news, and he said that he had plenty. He started to tell him about all that had happened to him since he drove out the cows that morning and about the coldness of the sea through which they had swum. The man of the house said that that sea was Death. When he told about the wall of fire and the healing well, the man of the house said that the fire was the fire of Hell, and that the well was for cooling and healing. 'If you have any drop of its water,' said the man of the house, 'take it with you for it has healing power.'

The son of the King of Sunday then told him about the cattle, thin as goats, that were in the field of rich grass. The man of the house explained that the thin cattle had been married couples, who had their seven sufficiencies of the world's goods and yet had been dissatisfied and quarrelsome; the fat cattle, he said, had been couples who, despite their poverty, had been satisfied with their lot. When told about the man with the dirty nose, who had been tied to a gate, until released, the man of the house said that that man had been in Purgatory and could only be released by somebody from this world cleaning his nose. The son of the King of Sunday then told him about the pieces of apple which the cows had eaten, about the Mass-bell and the Mass, and about the priest who sweated blood, which was wiped away by the clerk, during the Mass.

'The priest who was sweating blood during the Mass was Our Lord,' said the man of the house, ' and I was the clerk who was drying the blood off him. I am Saint Joseph. It wasn't with any evil intent that I brought your sister here. The Devil was trying to get her, but he wouldn't do the work on a Sunday, for he doesn't want to have anything to do with that day. I did the work on the Sunday and saved her from him. You and your sister can return home now, with my blessing.'

When they were setting out for home, Saint Joseph gave them two towels to take with them; whenever they felt hungry, food would appear on the towels for them to eat. On reaching home, every kind of food appeared on the towels for them that night. And when they had eaten it, they both, in the company of their father, the King of Sunday, went up as angels through the roof of the house.

11 The Dry and Wet Funeral Days

THIS STORY IS OF A DIDACTIC character, pointing out how individuals may suffer because of wrong behaviour of some kind. Setting out into the world in search of answers to particular questions is a common motif in folktales, and their final resolution brings the tales to an end. Each of the wrong-doers in this particular story is an example which may be cited in moral teaching *(exemplum)*. In this version, however, they are fused into a long tale.

There was a married couple living in Glendowan one time. They had only one son. The father was a very good-hearted man, very kind and obliging to everybody. His wife was different. She'd be angry if even the crows perched on the farm! When the son grew to be a man, he was wondering at the difference there was between his parents. They both lived to a great age.

The father died at the beginning of summer. The weather had been very fine until the day he died, but it rained and stormed as hard as it could during the wake, and the people who attended the funeral were drowned wet when it was over. The son was surprised that this should happen to his father, who had been so good all his life, but he said nothing. After Christmas, that same year, the mother died. There had been very bad weather, with storm and frost and snow, just before that, but it changed the moment she died, and it became warmer than it would be in summer. The people who attended her funeral had to take off their coats on the way home from the graveyard, so warm was it.

When his mother was buried, the son decided to travel to see if he could meet anybody who could tell him why the weather was so different when his father and his mother died. You'd imagine he could find something better to do! He had a few cows and he asked a neighbour to look after them until he returned. He set out for the road early one morning and asked everyone he met could they answer his questions, but they knew no more than he did himself. When night came on him, he went into a house at the side of the road. A widow and her three daughters were living there. He asked for lodgings until morning and was told that he would be welcome. The widow got supper ready, and when it was over, they sat around the fire, chatting. He told the woman why he was travelling around, but she couldn't help him.

'Here I am myself,' said she, 'with the three finest daughters in the whole country, and I can't get a husband for any of them. I don't know what is wrong. Maybe on your travels you could find out the cause of my troubles as well as your own?'

After his breakfast next morning, he set out on the road again and questioned everybody he met, until night came on. Nobody could help him. He came to another house by the road and went in. The married couple who were living there had no children. He asked the woman for lodgings until morning and was told that he was welcome to stay. She got the supper ready for himself and the man of the house. They ate it. An hour later, she had to get ready another supper for her husband, and still another before he went to bed.

'Isn't it a strange complaint I have?' said the man of the house. 'I'm still hungry, no matter what I eat!'

'There's such a complaint, all right,' said the traveller. ''Tis called the hunger complaint.'

'I went to a lot of doctors, but none of them could tell me what's wrong with me,' said the man of the house. 'As you're travelling on the road, you might be able to find out the answer to my trouble too.'

The following morning, he took to the road again, asking his questions of everyone he met, but it was all no use. He was as far from the truth as he was before! In the evening, he came to a slated house at the roadside. A married couple, with a houseful of children, were living there. He asked for lodgings and was told that he could stay till the morning. The woman got ready his supper. The man of the house was sitting on a chair in the middle of the floor, and a drop of water from the roof was constantly falling on his head. No matter where he sat, the drop followed him, even though there was no rain falling outside! The traveller told him why he was on the road and what questions he was asking.

'I have been here for seven years,' said the man of the house, 'and that drop is falling on the top of my head, summer and winter.'

'That's very strange,' said the traveller.

'As you're on the road,' said the man of the house, 'you might try to find out the cause of it?'

'I'll do my best,' said the traveller.

After his breakfast next morning, he walked on and kept going until a heavy shower of rain came on about dinner-time. He went for shelter under a cliff by the roadside, and stood under a tree that was growing on the cliff. There was a river running beside the road, and when he looked across it, he could see a woman at the other side. He hadn't seen her at all until then. He shouted across to her.

'Tell me, in the name of Jesus,' said he, 'did you live as a human being in this world? Are you still in this world, or have you left it?'

'I have left it,' said she.

'Well, if you have,' said he, 'you will be able to give me the information I'm looking for.'

'I'll tell you what you want to know,' said she. 'You're trying to find out about your father and mother.'

F

'I am indeed,' said he.

'Well,' said she, 'your father was a wonderfully good, hospitable man, and he left this world without a sin on his soul, I may say. There was only a small stain on his soul, and enough rain fell during his wake and funeral to wash it away. There was very fine weather, with great heat, when your mother was buried but that was nothing to the heat she has now!'

He walked on a little way and then returned to ask her about the people in the three houses he had spent a night in on his travels.

'Well,' said she, 'you can tell the man you were with last night that, if he takes in the poor orphans whom he banished from his door, the drop will cease to fall on the top of his head. And tell the man of the second house that, if he says Grace after Meals, his great hunger and thirst will stop. Tell the widow woman in the first house you stayed in that she is too proud of her daughters. If she gives that up, they'll get husbands.'

He thanked her and walked back to the house of the man on whose head the drop of water was always falling. He told him the reason.

'That's true enough,' said the man. 'We drove off some orphans from our door, but I'll bring them back here.'

He left the house and went to where the orphans were. He invited them to come back to him, but they refused. He returned home, but since he had asked them to come to him, the drop of water ceased to fall and never fell afterwards. The traveller then went on to the second man's house and told him what was causing his constant hunger. The man ordered his wife to get ready a meal for the traveller and himself. When he had eaten, the man of the house said Grace after Meals, and the hunger left him and never returned. Next morning, he set out for the house of the widow woman, who had the three fine daughters, and told her why they weren't getting husbands.

'So that's the reason!' said she. 'I suppose it was sinful of me to be so proud of them.'

'Well,' said the traveller, 'I'm the only person at home now. I have a good farm, and you should give me one of your daughters.'

'You'll get your own choice of them,' said the widow.

'I won't do any choosing. I'll take the eldest,' said he.

So he married the eldest, and within a year, the other two were also married. They all lived happily ever afterwards.

12 The Twining Branches

THIS IS A SAD STORY OF 'the sorrows of love'. Not that the love of either of the two persons concerned was not returned—that has been the theme of thousands of songs; in this case, however, the girl is forced by her father into an unwanted marriage and dies beside the body of her already dead lover.

The poetic lament (*caoineadh* or keen) which she composed extempore over her sweetheart was in true Irish tradition, when the deceased person, not necessarily a lover, was eulogised by the surviving relatives to a sad musical air.

Almost one hundred versions of this tale-type have been recorded in Ireland.

There was a strong farmer one time and he had plenty of money and land. He had only one in family, a fine handsome daughter. She fell in love with a local boy, who had very little of the world's riches; all he had, as the saying goes, was his shirt and breeches. The farmer was ashamed, when he met wealthy people like himself, at the idea of his daughter marrying such a poor fellow. As far as the two young persons were concerned, either would die if parted from the other.

The farmer had picked out, as a suitable husband for his daughter, a man who had money, and when the girl came of age to marry, her father sent for this fellow and his relatives, and a marriage-match was arranged. The girl didn't say Yes or No to her father, but let him have his own way, although her heart was as black as coal at the thought of parting from her true love. When the match had been made and the time fixed for the marriage, everyone around was invited to the farmer's house. The girl asked her lover to come also. When he heard that she was to marry another man, a dart of pain went through his heart, and he took to his bed. He felt that it would be better for him to be dead. The night that the marriage-feast was being held in the girl's house, he was dying with sorrow in his own house. The girl was unhappy that he didn't come to the feast.

At that time, the marriage would always take place late at night, when the feast was over. The priest would marry them in the house. The girl and the fellow whom her father had chosen were married, and soon it was time for everyone to go to bed. But, if it was, the girl was hesitating and busying herself with this and that and small chores. The bed had been made since noon the day before, but, if it was, she wasn't getting into it. Her husband was in bed, but she stayed up all night. And before the day dawned, word was brought that her lover had died.

The young husband got up in the morning and ate his breakfast along with the farmer at the same table. Then the farmer tackled his horse under the cart and threw a large armful of hay into it. His daughter went out to him.

'Where are you going to, father?' she asked him.

'To the corpse-house,' said he.

'I suppose my mother will be going with you,' said she.

'She will,' said he.

'I suppose you wouldn't let me go with you,' said she.

'I won't,' said he. 'Stay at home. 'Tisn't right or proper for you to go to a house like that today. Stay at home, I say. Stay with the man who is married to you and mind him. That's your duty now.'

When they were ready to leave, the farmer sat into the cart and so did his wife, and off they went. They had to go to the corpse-house by a roundabout way, but there was also a short-cut leading to it. As soon as the cart had gone out of sight, the daughter threw on her cloak and went by the short-cut, so that she was there before her father and mother drove into the yard with the cart. The farmer untackled the horse and he and his wife went into the house. They went on their knees beside the corpse and said some prayers. Then they stood up and sat somewhere.

There was a lone woman with a cloak over her head keening and lamenting loudly over the corpse, and the farmer was very troubled, as he thought her voice was like that of his daughter whom he had left behind him at home. He was wondering was it she or how she got there. When the woman was worn out from keening and crying, she wailed aloud:

' You are my love and my dear one,
And a good sign of your manhood

Was your strength and activity, your jump and run,
And your swift turn at sea.
You are my treasure and my loved one.
Last night I was married to a man;
Good are his qualities,
Well can he read
A book of Latin or of English.
But I won't lie down at his side
Until I go under the clay with you!
You are my love and my dear one,
And often you and I
Were inside at the edge of the grove,
Your fair head on my breast;
How sweetly I kissed you,
No more sweetly than you kissed me.
But there's another explanation for that—
The men and the women won't believe it.
I bid ye all goodbye now,
And I'll go under the clay with this man.'

She said no more. Everyone was wondering. They were all silent, but not another word or cry came from the woman. The farmer knew that the woman was his daughter. He stood up and went over to her as she bent over the table under which the corpse was laid out. When her father lifted her up, he found that she was dead.

The house was filled with talk and commotion when the girl was found to be dead. When the father was getting ready to take her body home to his own house, some sensible people who were at the wake said that it would be wrong to separate, when they were dead, two persons who were so close to each other when alive. They said that the two bodies should be buried in the one grave. The farmer was a headstrong man, and he wouldn't listen to them at all. He said that his family had a tomb, and in it she would be buried. He took her body home, and she was waked that night. Her father and mother were crying and lamenting, and no wonder, their fine daughter who was married the night before and was waking the next night, and she their only child.

The two bodies were to be buried in the same graveyard next day, at opposite sides. Some people went to the girl's father again on the day of the funeral and said that two persons like them, one of whom had died because of the death of the other, should be put into the same grave. But the stubborn father wouldn't agree to that. So they were buried at opposite sides of the graveyard. They weren't long buried when a tree grew up out of each grave, and they weren't grown very tall before they bent towards each other and became entwined. They embraced each other until they looked like a single tree. They were plainly to be seen in the graveyard at Aghadoe, near Killarney.

Sean Slammon's Dream (see page 94)

III Legends and Folk Belief

13 Fated to be Hanged

THE INTRODUCTION TO THIS TALE, where, by viewing the stars, a prophecy is made concerning the fate in store for the child who has been born at a particular time, often occurs in folktales. The child may, as in this case, be fated to hang or, in others, to drown, or to be consumed by a monstrous reptile (the Devil) or to suffer an unusual death in various ways. In most cases, as here, the evil fate is averted through the holiness or other good qualities of the fated person. An example of this is Type 934 (The Prince and the Storm)—that number cannot, however, be applied to the following story.

There was a farmer one time, and at twilight, one evening, there came into the house to him a young man who was dressed like a priest. He asked the man of the house for lodgings.

'You'll be very welcome,' said the man of the house, 'but I must tell you how we are fixed tonight. My wife is expecting a baby, and you mightn't have a very restful night.'

'I'll be all right,' said the traveller. 'I'll sleep here on the settle.'

Later on in the night, the midwife came down into the kitchen from the bedroom and told them that the baby would soon be born.

'When the time comes,' said the traveller, getting up off the settle, 'tell me.'

When the midwife told him later on that the baby was about to be born, he asked her to delay the birth.

'For how long?' asked the midwife.

'Five minutes,' said the traveller.

'I can't delay it even one minute!' said the midwife.

'The baby is being born under the planet of hanging!' said the traveller.

The baby was born, and the traveller stayed until morning. When he had eaten his breakfast, he pulled a pen and a book out of his pocket and wrote something on a page.

'Now,' said he to the man of the house, 'tie this piece of paper around the baby's neck and don't let anyone alive open it until he can read it himself.'

The man of the house did as he was told. The traveller then went to the room and said goodbye to the mother before leaving. The child got good care and wanted for nothing, and when he grew older he went to school. His name was Sean. One evening like this, when he came home from school, he asked his mother why this thing was hanging around his neck. The mother told him, word for word, about the traveller the night he had been born.

'If you're able to read it, there's nothing to stop you,' said she.

He opened the paper and read it, and what was on the paper

was that he had been born under the planet of hanging. He folded the paper up carefully and tied it around his neck as it was before. When he grew up to be a man, he took good care of himself and did nothing that would darken his soul. He left home, the poor man, and went to County Limerick. He got work from a farmer, and was a good, diligent worker. Another servant-boy slept in another bed in the room with him, and one night, the other fellow noticed Sean getting out of bed and pulling on his trousers. Sean then went down the stairs and out by the door. The same thing happened the following night, so the other servant-boy told the farmer about it.

'Now,' said the farmer, 'if you notice him doing that tonight, tell me.'

The farmer and the two men worked away during the day, and after a while, Sean began to yawn.

'It looks to me, Sean,' said the farmer, 'that you didn't sleep last night.'

'I didn't sleep much, then, or the night before that either,' said Sean. 'There's no terror but the dream I had for the last two nights! I dreamed that I was on the gallows and was hanged!'

That night, as soon as the companion felt Sean leaving the room, he called the farmer.

'Now,' said the farmer, 'follow him wherever he goes, step by step, and I'll follow you.'

They followed Sean, step by step, till he reached the church. He went in, followed by the servant-boy and the farmer. The church was full of light, to their surprise, and as soon as they went in, the pair of them went on their knees inside the door. Sean went up to the altar. Two angels descended, erected a gallows on the altar, and hanged Sean. Sean rose up then, walked down the church and went out the door. As soon as he left the church, the lights went out. They returned home and went to bed. Next morning when Sean and his companion had eaten their breakfast, the farmer came into the kitchen.

'Well, Sean,' he asked, 'did you sleep last night?'

'I didn't, or a single wink, master,' said Sean. '"Twas the same as before. I dreamed that I was being hanged on the gallows.'

'And so you were!' said the farmer. 'You were hanged last night.'

The farmer and the other man told Sean about all that they had seen happening in the church.

'You are a saintly man, Sean,' said the farmer, 'and 'tisn't working like this you should be.'

The farmer told the story to the parish priest, and the priest did his best to help. Sean was sent to a college and he left it a priest before he died.

That's my story, and if 'tis a lie, let it be!

14 The Mouthless Child

THIS STORY IS THE 'STUFF' of an *exemplum* (moral tale told during a sermon); whether it has ever been used in this way is not known, however. Its basic idea is a didactic one: to prove that the breaking of tabus by acting in an insulting manner, for example, or by having a lack of trust in God, is liable to be punished, and that the nemesis may fall on a seemingly innocent relative. Such tales are known in many countries in Europe, and, being of a legendary nature, were believed to be true.

I heard a story about two sisters who lived in this district long ago. Both were married. One of them was a fine, handsome girl, and, when she came of age to marry, a rich man put his eye on her, and they got married. The other sister wasn't so comely, and she married a man who had a small patch of land near her home.

If the second sister wasn't good-looking and didn't get a rich husband, she was happy with her lot. She had a baby born to her each year after her marriage, and it went on like that until she had seven in all, four sons and three daughters. Her sister, who was married to the rich man, had no children at all, and she was very jealous of the other. Each time that the second sister had a baby, the other would visit her and scold her terribly for having so many children, poor as she was.

'Well,' the poor sister would say, 'it is God who has sent them to me, and He never yet created a mouth without providing enough food for it!'

Time passed, and a good while later, the rich sister gave birth to a child. When the poor sister heard the news, she was delighted and went to see her. When she reached the house and saw the child, she noticed that it had no mouth! She almost fell down in a faint when she saw this.

'Now, sister,' said she, 'you were scolding me for having too many children, without having a bite of food half of the time to put in their mouths. You see now that it is far worse to have plenty of food but no mouth with which a child may be fed.'

The rich sister didn't answer a word. Of course the child soon died. Her riches were not of much use to its mother. But the poor sister, who was often short of food, got on far better, and she and her children did well in the world.

15 Saint Colmcille and Tory Island

SAINT COLMCILLE ('Dove of the Church'), also referred to as Columba, was one of the most famous of the early Irish monks. He is said to have lived from 521 to 597. Born in Gartan in County Donegal, he founded many monasteries in Ireland and went to preach to the Picts in Scotland in 563. A large number of legends about him is found in his Life (written by Saint Adamnan), as well as in his Life *(Betha Coluimb Chille)*, by Manus O'Donnell, written in 1532. Many of these legends are still current in Irish oral tradition.

In old times, when Tory Island, off the coast of Donegal, was under a magic enchantment by the pagans, a great number of saints came to Donegal to break the spell. Each of them spent a while in Gweedore, on a hill-top, looking out towards where Tory was lying, but they couldn't catch any sight of the island. The hill came to be known as the Hill of the Saints, and that's its name to this day.

At last Saint Colmcille came and he stayed in a thatched house at the foot of the hill. There was a servant-boy in the house who used to be herding cattle every day on the hill. One day, he was standing on the hill, looking out towards the sea, and he saw Tory away in the distance. He ran to the house and told this to Colmcille, and the two of them went up on the hill. They walked to and fro but couldn't see the island.

'If you are here tomorrow,' said Colmcille, 'and if you see the island again, stick your staff into the place you are standing on, and it will be a mark for us.'

The following morning, the boy was herding on the hill again, keeping a sharp eye on the sea, and at last he caught sight of the island again. He stuck his staff into the sod that was under his feet and came to the house to tell Colmcille that he had seen Tory again. But no sooner had he stuck his staff in the ground than the people in Tory knew that he had done so. The king and queen of Tory went from there to the mainland, and when they were within two yards of the shore, the king threw a stick from the boat and said:

'May your like be on every sod of ground here as far as the hill-top!'

When Colmcille and the boy reached the place, there was a thick wood of staffs covering the place as far as the top of the hill.

'I see that there was somebody hard at work since you left here,' said Colmcille to the boy, 'so we won't be able to find the right sod of ground.'

They pulled up the staffs, and Colmcille asked the boy, if he were there again tomorrow and saw the island, to make the sign of the Cross over the sod on which he would be standing, and to stick his staff into the spot.

'If you do that,' said he, 'the Tory people won't be able to come next or near the place.'

Next day, the boy was herding as usual and looking out towards where Tory was lying, and he saw the island again. He made the sign of the Cross over the spot, as he had been told to do, and stuck his staff into the ground there. He ran down to tell Colmcille the news. When they came back to the spot, they could see Tory quite clearly in the distance. Colmcille then went down to the harbour and got a boat-crew of the O'Friels to take him to the island. When the people of Tory saw the boat approaching, they all gathered on the strand, and the king shouted that he would not allow anybody to set foot on his kingdom. Colmcille answered that he wasn't asking permission to land on the island; all he asked for, he said, was to be allowed to rest himself on a rock at the shore.

The king gave his permission for that. Colmcille left the boat, taking his cloak with him. He spread out the cloak on the rock and sat down on it. The cloak started to spread out and out, and the people ran in fear before it until it forced them over the cliffs into the sea. The three Sons of Gor were the last to leave the island. They faced towards Aranmore and, when they reached half-way, they turned around and spat towards Colmcille. He turned them into three rocks, and they are there to this day. It is said that they set sail for Tory once every seven years on May morning, and if they could reach the island they would set it ablaze. But if a Tory man happens to catch sight of them coming, they must return to where they left. A poisonous hound was the last animal to leave Tory at that time, and the trace he left on a rock there is to be seen to this day.

Colmcille sent three people named MacRory to take possession of Tory and to live there, and he gave permission to the O'Friels, who had brought him in their boat to the island, to lift the Tory clay—any house which has some of that clay will never have a rat in it!

After spending some time on Tory, Colmcille returned home to his native place, Derryveagh. He afterwards stayed for a while in Downpatrick in County Down. He was opposed to English law in Ireland, so he was arrested by the English and sent to prison in Scotland. There is an island south of the Highlands where he was, and from there every clear day that came, he could see Ireland away in the distance. He was then sent inland so that he could not see Ireland any more. Each day as he walked about, he would sit down near the shore and ask one request of God: that he would never die in Scotland.

The following summer as he was walking near the strand one day, he saw a sod of turf being washed towards him by the waves. He recognised that it was a sod of Irish turf, and the thought struck him that his end was near. He sent word to the bishop, and when he came, Colmcille told him about the request he had made to God. The bishop heard his confession and anointed him.

'When I die,' said Colmcille, 'lay out my body and place it in a coffin, and I will reach one of the three places where I am to be buried, Tory Island, Derryveagh or Downpatrick.'

He sat down on his chair and placed the sod of turf beneath his feet. That's how he died. His body was placed in a coffin, and when it was closed, it was left to drift with the sea. The bishop sent word to the people of Ireland to be on the watch for the coffin. On the third day, it arrived at the mouth of Lough Swilly.

Great contention then arose between the people of Derryveagh and the people of Downpatrick as the which of them would get the saint's body. Each of them wanted to have it for burial in their own place. The decision that the bishop of Derry at that time made was that a carpenter should be ordered to make a coffin exactly like Colmcille's, and that the two coffins should be placed in a dark room. Each of the contenders could then take the coffin they chose and bury it in their own graveyard. That is what was done.

And it is said that when the coffin that was taken to Downpatrick was laid down beside that of Saint Patrick, he stretched his hand out of his own coffin to welcome Colmcille. That's how they knew then that Colmcille's body had gone to Downpatrick!

16 Sean Slammon's Dream

DREAMS IN GENERAL ARE AN important and rich theme in Irish oral tradition. The variety is seemingly endless: dreams which are regarded as omens of good or bad luck; those in which real happenings are enacted and are later proved to have been true; dreams of hidden treasure and the like; how dreaming of unhappy things may be averted, and so on.

In the following story, Sean Slammon, who said that he had never yet dreamed, is induced by over-eating, not only to dream but to have a fantastic nightmare, which ends when he finds himself in an uncomfortable position, hanging on to the chimney-crook of the house in which he slept rather than to the sky-borne flail of which he was dreaming.

Although nightmares can be frightening and terrible for the dreamer, stories such as this were told in a humorous vein and were not to be taken as having been really true.

In Irish folk tradition there was a well-known and often recited prayer *(Ortha an Tromluí: The Charm against Nightmares)*, which people recited before retiring to bed.

In the olden times, there was a man living near the churchyard of Downpatrick, in the parish of Caherlistrane in County Galway. His name was Sean Slammon. He made his living by tanning leather. He had a good deal of money but that didn't make people look up to him, because his trade was a dirty one, they thought. There was another man living near him, at the foot of Knockma, named Dermot Kennedy. Dermot was a weaver of coarse flax. He too had a good deal of money, but the people didn't look up to him either. One day the pair of them met.

'Well, Dermot,' said Sean Slammon, 'you have plenty of money.'

'I have some,' said Dermot.

'I have a good lot of it too,' said Sean Slammon.

'I'd say that you have,' said Dermot.

'The people aren't looking up to us on account of the dirty trades they think we have,' said Sean Slammon.

'I think that's so,' said Dermot Kennedy.

'Twould be better for us to take on some other kind of trades,' said Sean.

'If you think it better,' said Dermot, 'we'll start buying and selling cattle. I wouldn't mind doing that.'

'There'll be a fair in Turloughmore tomorrow,' said Sean. 'We'll go there and buy a few sheep.'

'Very well,' said Dermot.

They got up fairly early next morning and set out for Turloughmore. They bought a score of sheep and a small, grey wether.

'There'll be a fair in Galway tomorrow,' said Sean, 'and we may as well drive them west to Galway and make a bit of profit on them.'

'I don't mind,' said Dermot

They went along the road towards Galway, driving their sheep. It was late in the evening as they were passing through Claregalway, and the little wether couldn't keep up with the rest of the flock. They went into the house of a farmer by the side of the road and asked for a field to put the sheep into for the night and lodgings for themselves. The man of the house gave them what they asked for, and welcome. The little, grey wether was exhausted by that time, so they drew its blood and skinned it. They put down pieces of the flesh in a pot on the fire for their supper, and ate their fill of it along with the people of the house. They had driven the rest of the sheep into a field, so after their supper, they sat around the fire, telling stories. The talk came around to dreams.

'That's one thing I never did is dream,' said Sean Slammon.

'Would you like to have a dream?' asked the man of the house.

' I wouldn't mind at all, to see what 'tis like,' said Sean.

' Well if you follow my advice,' said the man of the house, ' I'll have you dreaming before morning.'

' I'll do what you want me to do,' said Sean.

' Put the four quarters of the little, grey wether into this bag, along with the skin and the tallow, and put it under your head as a pillow in the bed until morning.'

' I don't mind doing that,' said Sean.

' I'll go bail that you'll have a dream before morning.' said the man of the house.

He made a bed for the pair of them in the corner of the kitchen beside the fire, and they got into it for the night. Sean had his pillow under his own head: the four quarters of the little, grey wether, the skin and the tallow in a sack.

Sean began to dream that he awoke fairly early next morning and went out to see the sheep while the breakfast was being made ready. Whom did he meet but the son of the King of Leinster, he thought!

' Good day, Sean Slammon! Are those gloves you are wearing?'

' No,' replied Sean. ' They are the four quarters of the little grey wether, his skin and his tallow, all on account of trouble that came upon myself and Dermot Kennedy, coming from the fair of Turloughmore and preparing to go to the fair of Galway today!'

' You must take a letter from me to the son of the King of Scotland,' said the son of the King of Leinster.

' I'll be late for the fair so!' said Sean.

' I don't care. You must take the letter to him!' said the son of the King of Leinster.

' Give it to me quickly then!' said Sean.

He got the letter, and off he went to give it to the son of the King of Scotland. As he was passing by the old monastery at Claregalway, there was an old monk standing at the gate who hadn't walked a step for the past seven years.

' Good day, Sean Slammon!' said the monk. ' Are those gloves you are wearing?'

' No,' said Sean. ' They are the four quarters of the little grey wether, his skin and his tallow, all on account of trouble that came upon myself and Dermot Kennedy, coming from the fair of Turloughmore, and I must take a letter from the son of the King of Leinster to the son of the King of Scotland!'

' You must take me on your back,' said the monk, ' and carry me to the monastery at Urlar to say Mass and carry me back again here to Claregalway!'

'I'll be late for the fair at this rate!' said Sean.

'I don't care. You must do what I ask!' said the monk.

'Very well!' said Sean. 'Get up on my back quickly!'

He took the monk on his back and off he went, and he never stopped till he reached the monastery at Urlar. The monk said Mass there, and Sean carried him back again to Claregalway. That was that! Off he went then with the letter, and he had gone only as far as Leacht Seoirse when he met the Red Fox of Kesh.

'Good day, Sean Slammon!' said the fox, 'Are those gloves you are wearing?'

'No,' said Sean. 'They are the four quarters of the little grey wether, his skin and his tallow, all on account of trouble that came on myself and Dermot Kennedy, coming from the fair of Turloughmore, and taking the monk from Claregalway to the monastery of Urlar, and now I must take a letter from the son of the King of Leinster to the son of the King of Scotland!'

'Maybe your legs are taking you into danger!' said the fox.

'How's that?' asked Sean.

'That letter might be asking him to cut off your head,' said the fox.

'That might be true for you!' said Sean.

'Give me the letter till I read it!' said the fox. 'You can't read it yourself, can you?'

'I can't' said the man.

He gave the letter to the fox and he opened it. He started to read it, and he had only read three words of it when he heard the baying of hounds coming towards him.

'O, Sean!' cried the fox. 'Here are the hounds coming after me! I killed a couple of geese in the townland over beyond last night.'

The fox jumped up on the fence.

'Give me my letter!' cried Sean.

'I won't till I know what's in it!' said the fox.

Off ran the fox, and Sean after him, and the fox never stopped till he reached Tón an Chroic, above Claregalway. Sean kept close at his heels until the fox ran into a badger-hole. Sean didn't know what to do next. Then he remembered that he had heard about a man called O'Connor of Sligo, who had a pack of hounds and two terriers. Off he ran, and never stopped till he came to

O'Connor of Sligo, to borrow the hounds and the terriers to catch the fox and take the letter from him.

'I won't give you the hounds and the terriers,' said O'Connor of Sligo, 'until you get a letter of recommendation from your parish priest and from two justices, saying that you are a suitable man to get them.'

That was that! Sean had to return to his own parish, and the priest gave him the letter of recommendation. He then set out for the house of old Blake, a justice who lived at Cregg, and got another letter from him. Then he went to Ffrench of Cloonakalleen, another justice, and got a letter from him. He took the letters back to O'Connor of Sligo and got the hounds and the terriers from him. Back he went to Tón an Chroic with them. The terriers went into the hole after the fox, and the hounds stayed outside. Sean slipped off his shoes. The terriers were going along underground, and Sean and the hounds kept pace with them overhead, and Sean was such a good runner that the hounds couldn't keep up with him. The badger-hole where the fox and terriers were ran like a cave under the ground, and the exit at the other end was in County Clare. The chase continued until the fox emerged from the badger-hole in County Clare. He still held the letter in his mouth. Sean ran after him.

'Give me my letter!' he shouted.

'No, Sean, not until I know what is in it,' answered the fox.

Sean ran after him as fast as he could. In his hurry to get out through a gap, the fox dropped the letter from his mouth. Sean snatched it up and didn't trouble himself with the fox any longer. He returned to the hounds and terriers, and never stopped until he brought them back to O'Connor of Sligo.

'Well done!' said O'Connor of Sligo.

Sean started off again with the letter and never stopped until he handed it to the son of the King of Scotland.

'I'm afraid I'll be late for the fair!' he cried, as he ran back towards Galway.

He was travelling as well as his legs could carry him, when he met a shepherd on a road that lay between two hills.

'Good day, Sean Slammon!' said the shepherd.

'Good day!' answered Sean.

'Are those gloves you are wearing?' asked the shepherd.

'No,' said Sean. 'They are the four quarters of the little grey wether, his skin and his tallow, all on account of trouble that came on myself and Dermot Kennedy, coming from the fair of Turloughmore, and meeting the son of the King of Leinster and the monk from Claregalway and the Red Fox of Kesh and O'Connor of Sligo and his hounds and terriers, and now I must go to the fair of Galway today!'

'If you don't hurry, you'll be drowned, Sean!' said the shepherd.

'How is that?' asked Sean.

'I'll tell you,' said the shepherd. 'Once every seven years a flood rushes down from those two hills, and I think we won't have long to wait now.'

Sean ran off as fast as he could, and it wasn't long until the water started to pour down the mountainside. First it reached up to his ankles, then to his armpits. Sean caught sight of a boulder of rock and made his way towards it. He got up on top of it. The water kept on rising until it reached his ankles again on top of the rock; then it rose to his knees and soon reached his armpits.

'I'm drowned at last!' cried Sean.

An eagle came flying over his head.

'Good day, Sean Slammon!' said the eagle. 'Are those gloves you are wearing?'

'No,' said Sean. 'They are the four quarters of the little grey wether, his skin and his tallow, all on account of trouble that came on myself and Dermot Kennedy, coming from the fair of Turloughmore, and meeting the son of the King of Leinster and the monk from Claregalway and the Red Fox of Kesh and O'Connor of Sligo and his hounds and terriers and the son of the King of Scotland, and now I'm drowned at last!'

'I'll be able to save you,' said the eagle, 'if you give me my fill of that tallow on your back to eat.'

'I'll give it to you, and a thousand welcomes!' said Sean.

The eagle ate his fill of the tallow.

'Get up on my back now, Sean,' said he.

The eagle pressed himself in between Sean's two legs and lifted him up above the flood.

'Upon my word, you're a heavy bucko, Sean Slammon!' said the eagle. 'I'll drop you down again!'

'If you do,' cried Sean, 'I'll be drowned!'

The eagle continued to carry him high up until she touched the sky. She started to crush him against the sky, and Sean was so hurt that he began to scream. There were two men above the sky in Heaven, threshing oats with flails, and they heard the screams.

'What's making all that noise below us?' asked one of them. He put out his head to look.

'Ah,' said he, ''tis that bucko, Sean Slammon! He's riding on the back of an eagle!'

'Push out your flail and throw him off!' said the other thresher.

The first thresher pushed his flail under Sean and the eagle flew off. Sean took hold of the striking stick of the flail.

'Let go my flail!' shouted the thresher.

'Indeed, I won't!' said Sean. 'I'd be killed or drowned!' He kept his hold on the flail.

'Pull out your knife,' said the second thresher to the other, 'and cut the thong! Let the other half of the flail go with him!'

With the dint of fright and terror, Sean awoke from his dream. Where did he find himself but holding on with his hands to the iron hook in the chimney on which the people of the house used to hang the pots over the fire! Dermot Kennedy was fast asleep in the bed in the corner near the fire.

Sean had his fill of dreaming for ever more. He roused Dermot Kennedy, and the two of them went off to the fair of Galway. They returned home in the evening, merry and satisfied.

17 *The Fairy Frog*

FAIRY BELIEF WAS VERY STRONG in Ireland. The fairies were said to live in the 'fairy forts' (ring-forts which were the abandoned sites of farmsteads in former times). The present tale of the pregnant fairy woman in the guise of a frog was very popular. The belief that the fairies could take nursing mothers and babies (mainly males) into the 'fort' gave rise to hundreds of stories. In some tales, the abducted mother could be rescued from the *slua sí* (the fairy host, much feared, who were said to carry out such abductions).

She was only a small girl, about fourteen or fifteen years of age. Her people had a cow and they told her to drive her to pasture one morning. She was herding the cow in a field, and there was nobody anywhere near her. When some of the day had passed, the girl went up on the highest hillock in the field. She started to hum a tune and to dance on the hillock. It wasn't long till she saw a frog coming up the hillock towards her—the biggest frog she had ever laid eyes on. The frog sat down on the hillock, looking straight into the girl's face. The frog had a very large belly and, for devilment, the girl said: 'Don't give birth to your load until I am with you!' The frog turned away from her and went off down the slope.

The girl went home and forgot all about what had happened. Just a month from that day, herself and her father and mother were asleep one night, when they heard the sound of a horse's hooves approaching the door. There was a knock at the door, and the voice of a man from outside asked that it be opened. The girl's father jumped out of bed and opened the door, and the finest gentleman he had ever seen walked in.

'I don't recognise you, sir,' said the man of the house.

'I don't blame you for that,' said the gentleman. 'I came to ask you to do something for me?' said he.

''Tisn't much I can do for you sir,' said the man of the house. 'I'm a poor man.'

''Tis for your daughter I have come. I want her for twenty-four hours.'

The father didn't like that, nor did the girl, who spoke from her bed and said that she wouldn't go with him.

'Ah, you will,' said the gentleman. 'I give my hand and word to yourself and to your father and mother that you'll be home here again safe and sound, within twenty-four hours.'

'Well, sir, I'll take your word,' said the father. 'She'll have to go with you for that length.'

'Thank you,' said the gentleman.

'Get up and go along with him,' said the father.

She rose with great reluctance.

'Good girl!' said the gentleman, taking her by the hand and leading her out of the house.

He caught hold of her shoulder and lifted her up behind him on the horse. He gave spurs to the horse and rode away, conversing with the girl.

'You need not have the slightest fear now,' said he to the girl. 'There's no need for it, for I'll bring you home, safe and sound, to your father and mother tomorrow night. Give the back of your hand to the first food that will be offered to you,'; said he; 'say that you won't eat it. But you may eat the second food that will be offered to you, and any food given to you after that won't do you any harm.'

They rode along until they reached a hill, in the side of which was a high, awesome cliff. It would surprise anybody. A door opened in the cliff, and they entered the finest court that ever rose to the sky. There were many people inside, moving around and chatting with one another at their ease. The gentleman and the girl walked through the crowd till they entered the central room of the court. There were three nurses there, tending a woman who was ill in bed. There was a huge fire blazing in the grate, with flames rising from it. The moment the two of them entered the room, the woman in the bed gave birth to a child. As soon as the baby was born, two of the nurses took it from the mother, and the third started to poke the fire, making a hole in it. The child was laid down into the hole in the middle of the fire, and, to the wailing of the mother, was covered up with the live coals.

The baby wasn't yet fully burned, when in came a man and a woman; the woman was carrying a baby in her arms. She handed it to the sick woman, who had just given birth to the other baby. The baby began to drink at the woman's breast. It was a baby from the human world whom the fairies had taken in order that the woman would suckle it—that's the way they abduct children. The other baby was roasting away all the time, until it was burned to ashes. They lifted up the remains and they fell apart like ashes. There was a very large trough, as big as a vat, by the side of the wall near the exit-door. They sprinkled some of the ashes of the baby on the water in the trough; it was full to the brim.

The girl who had been brought there by the gentleman watched everything with wonder. A table of food was then laid out, and the girl was invited to eat. She refused, saying that that kind of food would not suit her. She asked for different food, and this was offered to her. She ate it. The gentleman had not left the room during the whole time, and he watched the girl.

'Good girl!' said he, when she had eaten the second food.

Just then three pipers struck up music for dancing. The house was overflowing with people, men and women, but none of them said a word to the girl. When day broke, the crowd started to leave. As each man or woman went out of the room, they dipped their fingers into the trough and rubbed the water to their eyes. The girl saw them doing this. She spent the day in the house until it was almost night. The gentleman left the room ahead of her and put some of the trough-water to his eyes as he went out. The girl was at his heels, and she was wondering what she should do about the water; she decided to rub one of her eyes with it, and even if she lost the sight of it, she would still have the other eye.

'I may as well give you a present before you leave,' said the woman with the baby in the bed, 'since you were so kind as to come when I sent for you.'

The woman turned about in the bed, pulled out a silken little neck-shawl and handed it and a stocking full of gold and silver to the girl. She had barely done so when the gentleman re-entered the room.

'You had better get ready to leave,' said he to the girl. 'I will leave you safely back with your father and mother.'

As the girl was leaving the room, behind him, she dipped her hand into the trough and put some of the water to one of her eyes. When she went outside, the gentleman jumped on the horse, took the girl by the shoulder and lifted her up on the horse behind himself. He conversed with her as they went along, until they came to a wood, a good distance away.

'Did the mistress give you any present?' he asked.

'Faith then, she did, and I'm very grateful to her,' said the girl.

'I see,' said the gentleman.

They were passing by a huge tree in the wood, when the gentleman jumped down from the horse and lifted down the girl in his arms.

'Go now, like a good girl,' said the gentleman, 'and wind the little shawl around that tree.'

No sooner had she done so, than the tree split into two halves, as if a hundred men had torn it apart.

'Leave the little shawl there!' said the gentleman.

She left it there. They mounted the horse again and rode on.

'Did the mistress give you any other present?' he asked her.

'She did,' said the girl, 'a stocking full of gold and silver.'

'Very good,' said the gentleman. 'Now, as soon ever as you reach home, you must go to all the fine houses and shops, and change that money, for within six nights from now, every house that will have any of the mistress's money in it will be burned by next morning. But your own money will be safe. You must do what I have told you for your own sake.'

Within a minute they were at the door of her father's house. The father and mother were sitting by the fire talking about their daughter when they heard the sound of a horse's hooves approaching. The horse stopped at the door. The gentleman dismounted, took hold of the girl and placed her feet on the ground. He entered the house with her.

'Here is your daughter back to you now,' said he. 'I am very thankful to ye. Good night!'

He went out of the house. On the following day, when the girl got up, she went around to the big houses asking for change of her gold and silver. Before six days had passed, she had changed it all. On the sixth night, every house that had any of the fairy money in it was burned to the ground.

The girl started to buy land and cattle and she went to every fair, buying and selling them. She went one day to a very large fair far from her home, and it wasn't long before she noticed there people whom she had seen in the fairy court. They were moving here and there through the crowds at the fair. She also saw the gentleman who had taken her from home and brought her back again.

'I must speak to him,' said she to herself, walking towards him through the crowd and shaking hands with him.

He shook her hand too.

'I'm very glad to see you,' said she.

'Wasn't it quick of you to notice and to recognise me?' said he. 'Did you see me with both eyes?'

'Oh, no, only with one,' said she.

'Might I ask you with which of your eyes did you see me?' he asked.

'Of course,' said she.

'Put your hand to the eye that you saw me with,' said he.

She did so. He immediately thrust his finger into that eye and tore it from her head.

'You won't see me any more,' said he.

And it was true for him. She never laid eyes on him again till she died.

That's how I heard this story I have told you. The dear blessing of God and of the Church on the souls of the dead!

18 The Cakes of Oatmeal and Blood

THIS RATHER RARE, AND GRUESOME story, has in its composition a number of motifs which are frequently found in other tales: the test-visit to a graveyard at night; the bearing of a dead (ghostly) man on one's back to a house; the power of a March cock to banish evil spirits at daybreak; and the discovery of hidden treasure. The main motif of the making of cakes with human blood and oatmeal and the subsequent resuscitation is, however, rare, or even unknown, except in versions of this story.

There was an upstart of a fellow one time, who was always arranging a marriage between himself and some girl, but in the end he never married any of them. He couldn't make up his mind which wife would be best for him. There happened to be a funeral one day, and after coming home, a little tipsy, he was invited to a dance in a neighbour's house. He went to the dance; there were lots of young men and women there, and some of his own relatives as well. They asked him had he any thought of getting married.

'I have, and every thought,' said he, 'but I don't know what kind of wife would be best for me.'

''Twould be better for you to marry me,' said one girl.

'Don't, but marry me!' said a second girl.

'I'd be a better wife than either of the two of them,' said a third girl.

'Well,' said he, 'I had a nice blackthorn stick with me, when I was in the graveyard today, and I left it stuck into the ground near the grave of the old woman we buried. I'll marry whichever of the three of ye will go there and bring me home my stick!'

'You may go to the Devil!' said two of the girls. 'We wouldn't go into the graveyard for all the sticks in the wood, not to mention your little, blackthorn one!'

'I'll go there,' said the third girl, 'if you keep your promise to marry me, if I bring you the stick.'

'I promise to marry you,' said he.

She set off for the graveyard, without any fear. She went into it and was searching around for the stick, when a voice spoke from one of the graves.

'Open this grave!' called the voice.

'I won't,' answered the girl.

'You'll have to open it!' said the voice.

She had to open the grave. There was a man in the coffin inside.

'Take me out of this coffin!' he ordered.

'I couldn't,' said she.

'You can very well,' said the man.

She had to take him out of the coffin.

'Now take me on your back!' said he.

'Where will I take you to?' she asked.

'I'll direct you,' said he.

She had to take him on her back and took him to the house of one of the neighbours, near her own. He told her not to go any further. She carried him into the kitchen. The family were all asleep. The man stirred up the fire.

'See can you get something for me to eat!' said the man.

'Yerra, where could I get anything for you to eat?' she asked. 'I have as little knowledge as yourself of the way about this house!'

'Go on! There's oat-meal in the room. Bring it here!' said he.

She found the room, and the oat-meal was there.

'See can you find milk anywhere now!' said the man.

She searched but couldn't find any milk.

'See is there water, if there isn't any milk!' said the man.

She looked everywhere for water, but there was none.

'There isn't a drop of water in the house,' said she.

'Light a candle!' said he.

She did so.

'Hold that candle for me now!' said he.

He made off to a room where two sons of the man of the house were asleep. He took a knife and cut their throats, and drew their blood. He took away the blood, mixed it with the oat-meal, and began to eat it. He urged the girl to eat it also, and when he came near her, she pretended to eat it, while at the same time she was letting it fall into her apron.

''Tis a great pity,' said she, 'that this should happen to those two boys.'

'It wouldn't have happened to them,' said the man, 'if they

had kept some clean water in the house; but they didn't, and they must take what has happened to them!'

'Is there anything to bring the two young men to life again?' she asked.

'No,' said he, 'because you and I have eaten what would have revived them. If some of the oat-meal which was mixed with their blood was put into their mouths, life would come back to them, as it had been before. And the two of them would have a good life, if they had lived,' said he. 'Do you see that field that their father owns?'

'I do,' said she.

'Nobody knows all the gold there is in it near the bushes over there,' said the man. 'You must take me back now to where you found me,' said he.

She took him on her back, and when she was going through a muddy gap which led out from the yard, she let the oat-meal which she had hidden in her apron, fall down near a fence. She took him along and never stopped till she took him to the grave out of which she had taken him.

'Put me into the coffin!' said he.

She did so.

'I'll be going home now,' said she.

'You won't!' said he. 'You must cover up my coffin with earth, as you found it.'

She started to fill in the grave, and after a while, the cock crowed at some house near the graveyard.

'I'll go now, the cock is crowing,' said she.

'Don't take any notice of that cock!' said he. 'He isn't a March cock. Work away and finish your task!'

She had to keep on filling in the grave. After another while, a second cock crowed.

'I'll go now,' said she. 'The cock is crowing.'

'You may go now,' said he. 'That's a true March cock, and if he hadn't crowed just now, you'd have to stay with me altogether.'

She went off home, and by that time, the dance was over. She went to bed, and slept late until her mother called her.

''Tis a great shame for you to be sleeping and the bad news we have near us at our neighbours!' said her mother.

'What news is that?' asked the girl.

'This neighbour of ours found his two sons dead in the one bed this morning!' said her mother.

'How can I help that?' asked the girl.

'I know you can't,' said her mother. 'But put on your clothes and go to the wake.'

She went off to the wake. She remembered every word that the man had said to her. All the people at the wake were crying, but she didn't cry at all.

'Would you give me one of them as a husband, if I brought them to life again?' she asked their father.

The young man who had sent her to the graveyard for the blackthorn stick was at the wake and he heard what she said.

'I thought you'd marry me,' said he.

'Don't talk at all!' said she. 'I'm tired enough after all I have gone through on account of you last night! Nobody knows what I have suffered on account of your blackthorn stick!'

'Joking me you are!' said the man of the house. 'I know well that you couldn't put the life into them again. I'm troubled enough without you making fun of me!'

''Tisn't making fun of you I am at all!' said the girl. 'I'll put life into them, if I get one of them as a husband, and all I'll ask along with him is that field above the house, the Field of the Bushes. You can give the rest of the farm to the other fellow.'

'I'd give you that field gladly,' said their father, 'if I saw that you had put the life into them again, as they were before.'

She went out and found the oat-meal that she had let fall near the fence. She took it in and put some of it into the mouth of each of them. As soon as she did that, the two of them rose up, alive, as well as they had ever been.

After a while, she married one of them and she told him the whole story about her meeting with the dead man. When they were married, she told her husband to go and dig near the bushes—that he might find something there. He did and found a potful of gold. He took it home and emptied the gold out of it, and put it into the bank or some other place to keep. The old pot happened to remain in the house, and there was some kind of writing on it that no one could read. A few years later, a poor scholar called to the house and he saw the pot.

'Who put that writing on the pot?' he asked.

'We don't know,' they said. 'We don't notice it much.'

'I don't either,' said he, 'but I know what the writing says.'

'That's more than we do,' said they. 'What is written on it?'

'It says that on the other side there is three times as much,' said he.

That put them thinking, and they remembered where they had found the pot and how much gold was in it. So when the night came, out went the girl and her husband, and they started to dig at the eastern side of where they found the pot. There they found three other pots, all full of gold! You may be sure that they weren't short of anything then! They built a fine house in the corner of that field. And that's how that girl got her money because of the man of the oat-meal.

19 The Spirit, The Sailor and the Devil

IN IRISH TRADITIONAL LORE, there are many stories about persons, supposed to be damned, who returned to earth in a ghostly form. They were of an evil nature, in most cases, and hundreds of stories tell of the attacks, often murderous, which they made on persons who happened to be out of doors late at night. Sometimes they could be overcome by the use of a black-handled knife, but in most stories, a priest had to intervene in order to banish the spirit. In the present story, the spirit is of a helpful nature and, by her advice, the sailor is saved from the Devil.

It is a good many years since there was this widow's son living north there in the parish of Ballyferriter. He was a hardy, strong, active, courageous fellow, and there wasn't any music or dance or amusement in any place that he wouldn't be at it. His poor mother used to be asking him every day what the devil was wrong with him, that he wouldn't stay at home and mind his home and farm.

'The day will come when you'll be sorry for the way you are carrying on,' she used to tell him.

He used to be out late and early and never felt lonely. Until one night, he was coming home from Dingle through the pass at Baile na n-Ath, a very lonesome place where something bad, a kind of spirit, used to be seen, and very late in the night, he met her. They faced each other, and she was getting the better of him in the struggle for a while. Then he noticed some kind of a necklace around her neck and, what the devil did he do but get his fingers inside it. She immediately became as quiet as a cat. He started to drag her along behind him, and she followed quietly until they reached a bridge.

'Where are you taking me now, good man?' she asked.

'I'm going to bring you to the priest,' said he. 'He'll put a stop to your travels and banish you from this place where you have been doing a lot of harm for a long time.'

'Widow's son,' said she, 'I'm miserable enough already! For God's sake, don't make me suffer any more, and my hand and word to you that I'll never again interfere with you or anyone else for the rest of your lives, if you let me go.'

'Well, I suppose it won't do me any good to put any other penances on you,' said he, 'and since I have got the upper hand on you and am rid of you, I'll let you go, even though you may never thank me for it.'

He let her go and returned home at the end of the night, tired out after his struggle with the spirit. Of course, his mother was accusing and blaming him as usual, but he didn't give her any account of what had happened. Two or three years after that, he went on board ship as a sailor, and after five or six or seven years he had risen, step by step, till he had a good position at sea, and finally owned a small ship of his own.

One day his ship was lying at the quay-side in Dingle. His crew had left him, so he wasn't able to take his vessel to some foreign country with a cargo, for want of a crew. In the evening, he saw, stepping down the quay towards him, a well-built, well-dressed fellow. They saluted each other.

'What's keeping you here so long, my good man?' asked the stranger. 'Your ship has been idle for a fortnight. Surely you could make some use of her instead of her lying here?'

'I can't get any sailors,' said the widow's son. 'My crew left me, and I'm trying to get another, but I'm still short of some men.'

'What pay would you give to someone who could do the work of seven sailors?' asked the stranger.

'I'd give you what you'd earn; that would be only fair,' said the widow's son. 'Wouldn't the wages of seven sailors satisfy you?'

'It would,' said the stranger. 'Be ready to sail at high-water tomorrow,' said he, 'and I'm the man will do the sailors' work for you.'

'I'll be ready,' said the widow's son.

When the bargain was made, the stranger went off, and the widow's son went into the town to get some things for the voyage. When he was on his way back to the ship, he saw a woman coming towards him as fast as a fairy-wind. He spoke to her.

'You were very worried for want of a crew for the past fortnight,' said she.

'I was, my good woman,' said he.

'I'd say you're for sailing tomorrow,' said she.

'I am,' said he. 'I ran into a man, and he bet that, if I gave him the wages of seven of a crew, he'll do all they could do. What more do I need?'

'He's well able for the work,' said the woman. 'But if he is, 'tis he that'll be asking pay from you, and not the pay you offered him. Your life won't be worth much when he'll be finished with you. Tell me, my boy, do you know who that man is? He's the Big Man himself, the Devil. And do you know who I am that's telling you this?'

'I don't remember ever having seen you before, my good woman,' said the widow's son.

'Do you remember the woman that you met one night years ago at the pass of Baile na n-Ath, and you caught hold of her necklace and were going to bring her to the priest?'

'I remember it well now,' said he.

'Well, I'm that same woman,' said she, 'and until today I haven't been able to reward you for what you did for me. Sail off tomorrow with your cargo. That fellow will do the work of a thousand sailors, but you must be able for him. When you have made your voyage and done your business, you'll be coming back here by way of the Skelligs Rocks. I'll raise a gale and great seas behind your ship by devilish magic. You must tell the sailor that the weather is changing and that there's a storm coming up, and that he must smear the cable with pure tar and soap and grease. As you come near this harbour mouth, I'll have raised a magic storm behind you. Then order him to let down the anchor lest the ship be wrecked against the rocks and ye both be drowned. He'll start to let down the anchor by the cable, and when the whole cable is out, except what he is holding of it between his two hands, order him to hold on to it or else to let it go. But he won't be able to let it go, because the gale and seas will be behind him. Go off now!' said she.

They parted then. The next morning at high-water, himself and the sailor set out to sea. There was never on a ship a man who was a better worker with spars and sails and tar and everything else. He did all the work perfectly. They did their business in the foreign country, took on board a new cargo and started on the voyage home in great friendship and comfort. When they were east of the Skelligs Rocks, the widow's son gave a look towards the south-west.

'I'm afraid there's a heavy storm coming near us,' said he to the sailor.

'There isn't,' said the sailor. 'Sure today is very fine!'

'Whether 'tis fine or not, 'tis my opinion that there's a gale of wind at hand.'

The wind started to rise and to blow hard and, if it did, the widow's son began to give orders to the sailor.

'Smear the anchor-cable with tar and soap!' said he.

The sailor did this. By the time they reached the mouth of Dingle Bay, the gale and seas were raging behind them.

'I'm afraid the ship will go on the rocks,' said the widow's son. 'Let down the anchor!'

The sailor started to let out the anchor-cable, with the ship racing through the foaming seas, until at last the only part of the cable that wasn't let out was what he held in his two hands.

''Tis all out except what I'm holding in my hands,' shouted the sailor.

'Hold on to it now, my man, or let it go,' said the widow's son.

Just as they were reaching the side of the quay at Dingle, the sailor let the cable go.

''Tis all out now,' said he.

The widow's son jumped on to the quay. The sailor raised his head and looked up at him.

'You have tricked me, fellow!' said he. 'Misfortune to the woman who taught you! I knew there was something about you that wasn't right.'

'Go to Hell now!' said the widow's son. 'I have that much satisfaction out of you. Long ago you should have got your deserts! Off with you now, and never come near me again!'

The Devil vanished and the widow's son made off to a public-house and, I suppose, drank a drop to give himself courage. I'd say that for the rest of his life he never took on a sailor like that again!

20 Seoirse de Barra and the Water-horse

THE BELIEF THAT THE SEA, lakes and rivers are inhabited by beings of human (mermaids and mermen), animal (horses and cattle) and other land-forms is to be found in the traditional lore of many countries. Stories are told of a busy world under the waters in which activities resembling those on land are carried on. It was considered dangerous for human beings to intrude into this marine world, however; stories such as that about Cluasach O Fáilbhe bear witness to this.

On the other hand, beings from the submarine world often intruded into the terrestrial one above. 'The man who married the mermaid' and the Melusine-type of story are illustrations of this.

The following tale describes how a water-spirit in the form of a horse came ashore and ultimately led to the death of the man who had captured and seemingly tamed it. This tale-type is known in many areas of Asia and Europe, especially in the north-western part of this continent. Various forms of the word 'nix' are applied to the water-horse. The more usual form of the story, unlike the following one, ends by the water-horse rushing into the lake, bearing its human rider on its back, and disappears; some time later, the liver and lungs of the drowned rider float to the surface. This motif is common in Ireland, Scotland and the Färoes, but is unknown in the rest of Scandinavia and Iceland.

In some versions of the water-horse tale, a line of famous race-horses descends from their sire. In most, however, the stallion returns to its watery home when wronged or ill-treated in some way.

For the place of the water-horse in Scandinavian tradition, see 'Some Notes on the Nix in Older Nordic Tradition', Dag Strömbäck, *Medieval Literature and Folklore Studies,* ed. J. Mandel and B. Rosenburg (Essays in Honor of Francis Lee Utley), Rutgers University, New Jersey, 1970, 245-56.

There was a man in County Mayo long ago. His name was Seoirse de Barra. He used to travel around Ireland, and he happened to come to the parish of Annaghdown, in County Galway. While he was there he got to know a young woman named Creeveen de Búrc, and after a while they agreed to marry. Each of them owned land in their native county.

After their marriage, they made up their minds to cross the seas, to see some of the great world. When they arrived in Galway to take ship, what should Seoirse see following him but a huge, white rat! Himself and the rat kept an eye on each other, and Seoirse felt that the rat had some design on him, maybe to kill him. The rat followed him on board the ship, and was always after him, wherever he went on the ship. It was the same when he landed in America; the rat followed him. Day or night, he couldn't escape from it, and he was afraid that it would kill him some night when he was asleep.

At last, he told his wife that it would be better for them to return to Ireland. If he was to die, he said, he would prefer to do so in Ireland than in America or anywhere else, far away from his own people. His wife agreed, and they returned home to Ireland. The rat was on the ship that brought them home, and was on the quay in Galway as soon as they were. Seoirse then made up his mind to take his wife to his old home in Castlebar in Mayo, where his brothers and his mother were living, so they took a coach for the journey.

One day, he was sitting near a fence at his home, full of worry and sadness. The big, white rat was sitting some distance away, looking hard at him. Up ran a weasel, and she attacked the rat. In the fight, the rat got the better of her, and she had to run off into a hole she had made under a mound of earth. After a while, she came out through the other end of the hole under the mound. Seoirse kept his eye on her and on the rat, and the rat never took his eyes off Seoirse. The weasel made another attack on the rat and made it so angry that it ran after her to the mouth of the hole. The weasel escaped inside, but all the rat could do was to put its head in through the opening. While it was trying to push its body in further, the weasel came out at the other end and took hold of the rat by the neck, and never let go her hold until she left the rat cold, dead at the mouth of the hole.

Seoirse jumped to his feet, thanking God and Mary and the weasel for his escape from the rat. He would be free from danger from then on, he thought. He ran into the house and called his wife, Creeveen de Búrc, and showed her the dead rat. As glad as he was himself, she was seven times as glad!

'Now,' said Seoirse, 'I'll never stop until I build a castle here where this rat was killed, and the name I'll give it is de Barra's Castle!'

'If you do that,' said Creeveen, 'I'll go to my own parish of Annaghdown in County Galway, and I'll build another castle where I was born and reared, and I'll name it Creeveen de Búrc's Castle!'

So they built the two castles. Seoirse's castle gave its name to the town of Castlebar in County Mayo, and his wife's castle in Annaghdown in County Galway is now called Creeveen's Castle. They lived from time to time in both castles.

There was a stretch of land to the east of Creeveen's Castle at Loughafoor. There were water-horses under enchantment in that lake and they were doing great damage to Seoirse's grain-crops by the shore. They used to come out of the lake each night and go into the corn-fields, and they had gone each morning before the sun rose. Seoirse asked all the men around to come every night for a week to try to come between the horses and the water when they would be returning to the lake before dawn. He wanted to catch one of them, for a wise, old, blind man, who lived in the district, had told him that, if he could catch one of them, the others wouldn't come any more.

Early one morning, Seoirse and the men went towards the lake, but the horses saw them and rushed out into the water. That night, the men went to the lake-side after their supper and lay down ahide, until they heard the horses coming. They remained between the horses and the water until day broke. The horses were in the corn-field, and the men tried to catch hold of a small, nice, young filly. They surrounded her and caught her, and brought her home westwards to Creeveen's Castle. They put her into a stable, and you never saw a little horse that was as nice or as quiet as her; she was getting more tame day by day.

Seoirse then told the old, blind man that he had a great longing to take her out hunting, but the old man advised him, if he wanted to have luck, not to take her out of the stable until a day and a year were past—the enchantment would then be over. Seoirse was counting the days until the time would be up, and thinking to himself that there wouldn't be as nice a hunting-horse in the whole country. But he didn't wait until the day and the year were up.

One day he decided to go riding on her east to Knockatoo, so that everyone in the country would see his lovely horse.

He rode on east, with his back towards the lake, and she went along as quietly as any horse you ever saw. When he reached the top of the hill at Knockatoo, he thought that it would be better for him to return home again; he was five or six miles away by then, and it would be fairly dark when he would be home. He turned the horse around on the road and faced westwards. She immediately caught sight of the water to the west, and as the enchantment hadn't yet left her, she wanted to be in the water and not on the land. Off she galloped, jumping and racing, and he was able to control her until she came to a place that they now call Leacht Seoirse. There she threw him off, and he was killed. The people saw the horse entering the lake, with the bridle and saddle still on her. They took Seoirse's body to Castlebar and he was buried there. I can't say that the bridle and saddle aren't still on the horse in the lake.

It was an old custom at that time, wherever a man or a woman was killed by accident, when people were passing the place, they would take up a stone and throw it on the heap of stones that was there, and they would say: 'The blessing of God on your soul, Seoirse de Barra!' Later on the heap of stones came to be known as Seoirse de Barra's Cairn in the parish of Claregalway, between Tuam and Galway.

21 The Conneelys and the Seals

IN THE FOLKLORE OF IRELAND and of other maritime countries there is a profusion of stories concerning seals. Possibly due to the fact that they can come ashore and that their head, when seen at a distance above the water, bears a resemblance to a human head, it was said that they were human beings under a spell. Some stories, like the following one, indicated that they had the power of speech. Stories of their origin varied.

The present story tells of the marriage of a seal-woman to a man; this is a very widely spread tale. The family-name of the man ranges from O'Shea in Kerry to Flaherty and Conneely and others in the West of Ireland, and to MacCodrum (relatives of the Gaelic poet) in Scotland. In some versions, the descendants of the seal-women were said to have webbed hands and feet.

All such stories end with the return of the seal-woman to the sea when she has recovered her cloak *(cochall)*, without which she would drown in the water. In Donegal there is a song in the Irish language ('The Song of the Mermaid') which is said to have been sung by the seal-woman as she met her children each morning at the sea-shore.

In the olden times, maybe a couple of hundred years ago, there was one family of Conneelys living in Errismore, very close to the sea. They had one son, a fine, young man. On May Day each year, three seals used to come ashore on a very big, flat rock that was high above the tide. There was a cave, five or six yards deep, at the back of the rock, under a cliff.

When the seals came up on the rock, each of them used to take off the hood that was tied about its neck and throw it into the cave behind them. As soon as they took off the hoods, they became the three finest women that the sun had ever shone upon, and they would go out swimming, each with a golden head of hair. The third woman was the most beautiful of all. When they grew tired after swimming for two or three hours, they would come back on to the rock again. Each of them would then take her own hood and tie it about her neck. She would become a seal immediately. After spending about a half-hour on the rock, the three seals would dive into the sea together and disappear from sight.

Conneely used to watch them every May Day, when they came. He liked the youngest woman best of the three, and wondered could he ever get her. He was working in the field one day at the end of Spring, when he saw, coming towards him, a fairly old man, whom he had never seen before. He spoke to the man, and they sat down to chat, each of them telling his own story. Conneely told about the three seals that used to come to the rock every May Day, and he pointed it out; he told everything about what they used to do when they came, until they dived into the sea again.

'There's one of them a lot nicer and more beautiful than the other two,' said he.

'I'd say that you have a liking for her,' said the man.

'Indeed, I have,' said Conneely. 'I'm in love with her, but I have no chance of ever getting her.'

'I have an idea who they are,' said the man. 'I have heard talk about them. What would you give to the person who would tell you the way you might get the one you want?'

'Oh, I'm only a poor man,' said Conneely. 'All I could give you as a reward is my seven thousand blessings.'

'That's a good reward,' said the man. 'I'll tell you what you must do. When next May Day comes, hide yourself in the morning in the cave, and when they throw their hoods into it, you must put the young seal's hood inside your shirt. Keep the other two hoods in your hands. The three women will be screaming and wailing, each of them asking for her own hood, and saying that their father will kill them, if they aren't at home by a certain hour in the evening. They are three daughters of the King of the Sea. You mustn't give the youngest woman her hood, at any price, no matter what screaming and complaining she has. Give the hoods to the other two. Then walk towards your house, and the youngest one will follow you. You must hide the hood in a place where she'll never see it. If she does, you'll have finished with her.'

'You may be sure that I'll never give her the hood,' said Conneely. 'I love her too much for that!'

The old man then stood up and left him, and Conneely never laid eyes on him again till the day he died. The time went by until May Day came, and at the dawn of day, Conneely hid himself in the cave. Later on in the day he saw the three seals coming up on to the rock. Each of them took off the hood, and threw it behind them into the cave, and they were the finest women that ever raised their faces to the sky. The youngest was the most beautiful of all. When the three women jumped in to swim, Conneely picked up her hood and shoved it inside his shirt, next to his skin; he kept the other two in his hands. He waited there until they came back to the rock. When they saw him with the hoods in his hands, they asked him for them, but he refused. They started to wail at the top of their voices, saying that their father would kill them, if they weren't home early in the evening. He threw her hood to the eldest, and the other two were still pleading for their own. He then threw the second hood to the second woman. The two seals jumped into the sea together and went off.

The youngest sister was left behind, and her cries would touch all the hearts in the world. He told her that he wouldn't give her the hood, and he asked her to go home with him. She had no desire to go with him, but at last she followed him to the house.

She spent the night there, and they got married next day. He hid the hood in the roof of the house, between the thatch and the sods. They lived happily together, and five sons were born to them. There wasn't a better worker than her to be found. But each day, when he would be out on the sea, fishing, she would weep her fill.

One fine, summer day, the husband was out on the sea, fishing, and his wife was working in the fields. Whatever look she gave towards the house, she saw that it was on fire. There were two or three other houses near it, and she shouted for help to quench the blaze. Two or three young men started to throw down from the roof the burning thatch, while she stood on the ground watching them. When a big forkful of the thatch fell down near her, she looked at it, and there was the hood in the middle of it! She rushed towards it, ran towards the sea and tied the hood about her neck. Immediately she was changed into a seal! She gave a jump into the sea and was gone.

Her five sons followed her to the shore but failed to find her. They returned home, crying for their mother. When Conneely returned home in the evening, the house was half-burned, his wife had gone, and the children were wailing for her. He sat down with them and he, too, cried his fill until morning. As soon as the children got up in the morning, they went down to where they had seen their mother go into the sea, hoping to see her. And they did. She came in close to the shore where they were and spoke to them. And there wasn't a day came during the next five years that they didn't go down to the sea, and she came every day and talked to them. When the five years were up, she told them that they would never see her again.

There were very few Conneelys in Errismore at that time. But you couldn't count all of them that descended from the five sons of the seal-woman. That's why they say that the Conneelys are related to the seals.

That's a true story, the way I heard it! If 'tis a lie, it wasn't I made it up. A blessing on the souls of the dead!

22 The Wounded Seal

THE FOLLOWING TALE, also about a seal (in reality, a human being under an evil spell) was recorded in West Kerry from Peig Sayers, who also told other stories to be found in this volume. She died in 1958, having been blind for some years, and a monument to her prowess as a storyteller was erected over her grave, facing westwards towards the Great Blasket island where she had spent most of her life, ten years later.

The motif of the evil stepmother, which occurs in this story, is very common in Irish folktales.

There was a poor woman there one time, and she had three children. Her husband died young, and she had to face the world as a beggar, with her bag under her arm, to try to rear the children. She travelled up and down, east and west through the country. She arrived at Dunquin and stayed a night in a house at Coumeenole. It was a Saturday night. On Sunday morning, the woman of the house got the morning meal ready for herself and the children.

'Don't be troubling yourself with us!' said she to the woman of the house.

'Oh, 'tis for the sake of the King of Sunday that I'm tending ye today,' said the woman.

They ate the breakfast.

'I may as well be starting out,' said the poor woman. 'Though 'tis early, I'm slow on the road, and I must go to Mass.'

She gathered the children around her and set out for the chapel. When she reached the top of the cliffs, she saw that the tide was a long way out below her. The sea was very calm.

'Let ye stay here,' said she to the children. 'Stay quiet while I go down and collect a handful of limpets and sea-grass.'

Down the path she went and started to loosen the limpets with a little piece of rock. She was on the outer end of a flat rock, with calm water on either side of her, and was picking the sea-grass, when she heard the water gurgling at the side of the rock. What was it but a big, grey seal, which was swimming in from the sea, and it never stopped till it came up on the dry rock between her and the shore! The woman stood up and felt very frightened, and no wonder. After a short while, she guessed that there was something ailing the seal, and when she looked at it more closely, she noticed that one of its paws was sore.

'I pity you, poor animal!' said she. 'You must be in great pain. I wonder can I help you in any way.'

She sat down on her haunches, pulled a pin from her skirt and started to pick out the hake-fin which had pierced the seal's paw. She kept picking until she took out the fin; then she pressed out the corrupt matter from the paw. When she had done that, she bent down and bathed the seal's paw in a handful of salt water. When the poor seal got relief from the pain, it looked between her two eyes at the woman, and she knew that it was the look of a human being, not of an animal. The seal soon slipped down from the rock and entered the water, but, before sinking, it turned its head towards her and shook it as if it were thanking her, before diving below the surface. When it had gone, she gathered up her little collection and returned to the cliff-top to her children. They were waiting for her, quiet and happy.

'Come now, little children,' said she; 'we must go to Mass.'

They made off the chapel, and when Mass was over, she went into a house and asked the woman there to boil the limpets for the children.'

'I will, and welcome, dear,' said the woman. 'This is Sunday evening; stay with us until morning.'

She stayed there until Monday morning; she then said goodbye to the woman of the house and they set out on their travels. She went up and down; the years went by, and the children grew until the eldest daughter was almost eighteen years of age. At that time, they were in the north of Ireland. A farmer's wife took the eldest girl as a servant. The mother and the two boys kept travelling on, up and down, as people like her did. Then one day in autumn, when the sun was shining down on them, there wasn't a house or a farm to be seen anywhere near them.

'I'm afraid, children,' said the mother, 'that we'll have to spend the night under the bushes. I can't see a sign of a house anywhere.'

After travelling another while, at last she saw a fine-looking house a good distance away.

'Hurry up, children!' said she. 'We might reach that house before night falls.'

They hurried on, and reached the house at last. She went in through the gate and stood at the door. She spoke gently to whoever was inside, and an old man, who was sitting on a chair in the corner, answered her kindly. He stood up, when she entered, went over to her and shook her by the hand. 'A hundred thousand welcomes before you, good woman!' said he.

'Long life to you, sir!' said she. ''Tis few people have any interest in an old woman like me!'

'Come up to the fire!' said he.

He took her hand and put her sitting on a chair in the corner; the two boys sat near her. He rang a little bell that was on the table, and it wasn't long till a servant came in. The old man ordered that food and drink be got ready for the old woman and her two sons. The meal was soon ready, and when they had eaten, 'Sit here in the corner again,' said the old man, 'and tell me about your travels and things you have seen.'

''Tisn't much I have to tell,' said the old woman, 'for people who are travelling like me don't pay much notice to things, except putting the day and the night over them.'

'All the same,' said the old man, 'have you seen any strange thing that struck you?'

She then started to tell him about the Sunday she took the hake-fin from the seal's paw near Dunquin, and how the seal had looked at her like a human being.

'That's the last I saw of the seal,' said she.

'Would you recognise it again, if you met it?' asked the old man.

'How would I recognise it, a poor animal in pain, from the sea?' said she.

'I'm that seal,' said the old man. 'I was the son of a gentleman, and my stepmother placed a spell and *geasa* on me. She turned me into a seal and, with her own hand, she struck the fin of a hake through my right hand. My hand festered and pained me until you picked out the fin. And now, I'm going to reward you. You have a daughter in service in a certain place. You must bring her here. I have one son here, and she'll get him in marriage. That's your corner there as long as you live. And your sons can be working around here. Neither you nor they will be short of anything for the rest of your lives.'

She brought her daughter to the house, and she and the son got married. They had a long, comfortable life together, herself and her family with the gentleman and his son.

23 The Fork against the Wave

THIS TALE-TYPE WAS VERY popular in Ireland, especially in the coastal districts. Inland, the scene of action was a lake. In most versions, the casting of the weapon (usually a knife or a spear) against a menacing wave on a stormy day was deliberate, rather than accidental, as in the present story. The sea-woman generally allows the man, who had cast and later withdrawn the weapon, to return home temporarily on condition that he comes back to her again. If he does not, he is usually swept out to sea by a mighty wave and disappears for ever. In the present story, too, it would seem that the 'woman in the wave' took the widow's son to her watery realm while his companions slept.

There was a widow's son in Iveragh long ago, and he had no fishing-boat or crew of his own. At that time, all the Iveragh fishing-boats used to come to the Blaskets to catch herrings. One day there was a boat at the pier in Iveragh, and the captain was short one of his crew. The widow's son happened to be standing there, and the captain asked him would he go to the Blaskets with them that night. He said that he would.

They started out, and were fishing for a while, when a storm came on, and they had to run for shelter between the Great Blasket and Illaunbwee. They were eating some boiled potatoes and meat in the boat, and the widow's son had a piece of meat on a fork, when the boat lurched, and in his excitement, instead of letting the fork fall inside the boat, he threw it and the piece of meat into the sea. As he did so, he caught sight, as he thought, of a woman in the wave. No sooner had he thrown away the fork, than the waves at each side of the boat subsided. They were safe then.

A night or two later, they went fishing in the same place, and all through the night they could hear voices through the sea, but couldn't see anybody. After a while one of the fisherman saw a small boat approaching, and it never stopped until it came alongside. There was one man in it, and he asked the captain would he allow the widow's son to go with him for a few hours. The captain said that he wouldn't, as he hadn't any authority to do so. He said that the boy was not one of his usual crew, and was only taking the place of a man who couldn't come. The captain and the crew then asked the widow's son would he go with the stranger. He said that he would, for a few hours.

'Now,' said the captain to the stranger, 'I'm giving you this boy, safe and sound, and you must bring him back to me as you got him.'

'I will, and welcome,' said the stranger.

The widow's son left his own boat and went into the strange, little boat. No sooner was he in it than the boat was out of sight of the captain and crew. They didn't know where it had gone to—

up or down, east or west. They went home, worried and arguing about what to tell the poor widow whose son had gone.

The little boat brought the stranger and the widow's son to the finest strand he had ever seen, with a wood on both sides of it, and a fine gravel road through it. The stranger led him to a fine court, where they saw a fine, young girl lying near the fire, with a fork stuck in her forehead.

'I'm this girl's father,' said the stranger, 'and I want for you to draw that fork from her forehead, for it was you stuck it there. But I warn you now that you mustn't draw a single drop of blood when you're doing it!'

The widow's son trembled in hand and foot, when he was warned not to draw any drop of the girl's blood, for he knew that he couldn't pull out the fork without drawing blood. He pulled out the fork and the piece of meat as slowly and carefully as he could, and not a drop of blood came. The girl rose up, as well as she had ever been.

'Now,' said the girl to him, 'if you stay with me, I'd give you this fine kingdom and court. It is you I was after the night of the storm, but when you stuck the fork in me, I couldn't take you with me.'

'I won't stay here with you,' said the widow's son. 'I'd rather go home to my mother and to my own home.'

'If that's the way,' said her father, 'come on and sit into the boat.'

They walked to where the little boat was and sat into it again, and they never stopped till the stranger handed him back to the crew.

'There he is for you now, safe and sound as when I got him,' said the stranger to the captain.

'Thank you very much,' said the captain.

The following week, the man that was missing from the crew returned, and the widow's son remained at home for a good while. Then one night, the widow's son joined the crew again, when the man was missing, and they were fishing for herrings at the same place, near the Blaskets. When the nets were let out, the rest of the crew fell asleep, and when they awoke, there was no trace of the widow's son. They had no account of him from that night on.

That's how I heard the story. I don't know whether it is true or false.

24 The Soul as a Butterfly

THE IDEA THAT THE SOUL OF a living person can leave the body during sleeping hours and wander elsewhere is found in the folklore of many peoples. Stith Thompson's *Motif-Index of Folk Literature* lists (E700ff.) the great variety of ideas concerning the human soul and the many forms which it was supposed to take. See the Notes to the following beautiful story ('The Guntram Legend'), in which the soul took the form of a butterfly, at the end of this volume.

There were two men searching for sheep one time in a glen. There was a stream running through it. They were tired and exhausted from their travels, so in the evening they stretched themselves down in the glen-side. The evening was delightful, and one of them fell fast asleep. The other remained awake. As he was watching the sleeper, he noticed his mouth widening, and out of it came a white butterfly! It went down along his body and along one of his legs, before alighting on the grass, and then went on for about six yards. The man who was awake rose to his feet and followed the butterfly until it reached a small, uneven pathway. It went along the pathway until it came to the edge of the stream. There was a stone flag, under which the water flowed, across the stream, and the butterfly went across by the flag to the other side. It continued on until it came to a small clump of sedges, and it went in and out through the clump several times. The man followed it for twenty yards or so further, until the butterfly came to an old horse-skull, which was white and weather-beaten. The butterfly went in through one of the eye-sockets, and the man watched as it went into, and searched, every corner of the skull. It then went out again through the other socket.

The butterfly then went back by the same route: in and out through the clump of sedges, across the stream by the stone flag; then along the uneven pathway, until it reached the sleeper's body. It made its way up along his right leg, and never stopped until it went into the sleeper's mouth. When it did this, the sleeping man closed his mouth. The next moment he sighed and yawned and opened his eyes. He glanced around and saw his companion looking at him.

'It must be late in the evening by now,' said he.

'Whether 'tis late or early,' replied his companion, 'I have seen some wonders just now.'

''Tis I who have seen the wonders!' said the sleeper. 'I dreamt that I was going along a fine, wide road, with trees and flowers at either side of me, until I came to a great river. Across the river was the finest and most ornamental bridge I had ever seen. Soon after crossing the bridge, I came to the most wonderful wood I had ever seen. I walked through it for a long time, until at the other side of it I came to a splendid palace. I went into it. There was nobody to be seen. I walked from one room to another until I grew tired. I was making up my mind to stay there, when an eerie feeling came over me. I left the palace and travelled along the same route home. I felt very hungry when I arrived, and then when I was going to eat some food, I woke up.'

'It looks as if the soul wanders around while the body is sleeping,' said his companion. 'Come with me now, and I'll show you all the fine places you passed through in your sleep.'

He told him about the butterfly, and showed him the uneven, little pathway, the stone flag across the stream, the clump of sedges and the horse-skull.

'That skull,' said he, 'is the fine palace you were in a while ago. That clump of sedges is the wonderful wood you saw, and that stone flag is the ornamental bridge you crossed. And that rough, little path is the fine, wide road you travelled, with flowers at every side!'

Both of them had seen wonders.

Cromwell and O'Donnell (see page 132)

IV Historical Tradition

25 The 'Danes'

FROM THE YEAR 795 until their defeat by King Brian Boru at the Battle of Clontarf, near Dublin, in 1014, Viking raiders made piratical incursions into Ireland. They settled in communities at various centres along the coast, and from these grew Dublin, Waterford and Limerick. The Vikings were popularly known in Irish tradition as the 'Danes', but the Irish term for them, *Na Loch-*

lannaigh: men of Lochlann (to be equated with Scandinavia), is a more correct title.

The practice by the 'Danes' of *jus primae noctis*, with which the following traditions begin, is frequently mentioned in connection with some landlords in Ireland.

The tradition that the 'Danes' had a secret recipe for the making of beer or ale from heather is widely known in both Ireland and Scotland. Experiments have shown, however, that the tips of the heather were probably used only as a flavouring for beer made from other ingredients.

Irish tradition also tells us that it was the 'Danes' who introduced foxes, weasels and hens into Ireland. It was said, perhaps jokingly, that they left the hens behind in Ireland for purposes of revenge—that they might tear asunder the straw roofs of Irish houses in their search for grains of oats or barley!

The old people of this townland used to say that the Danes were living here at one time, and a bad lot of people they were. It was from them, the old people used to say, that the old landlords learned their bad habits. It was the custom that, when a fine, young woman got married, she had to spend her marriage night with any Dane who would send for her, whether she liked it or not. Needless to say, the people were against this, but there was no use in talking about it, they couldn't prevent it. There were far more marriages taking place then than there are now.

The people were very dissatisfied and said it was time to put an end to that sordid practice. Just as there are now, there were at that time some clever people in Ireland, and one of them thought of a plan to kill a lot of Danes in a single night. There were some Danes, both men and women, married to Irish wives and husbands, and the plan was that every Irishman, who had a Danish wife, would kill her one night, and Irish wives would do the same with their Danish husbands. It had all to be done the same night, and not a word was to be said about it to anyone else.

The old people used to say that the Danes had a custom of leaving a light burning in their houses all night until morning—they must have had some lights of their own, since rush-candles wouldn't last until morning. Secret orders were sent out that each house in which a Danish man or woman was to be killed that night should keep the light burning until morning. The killing started about midnight, and all the Danes who were married to Irish people were killed. Their heads were cut off. The old people used to call that night the night of the treachery.

Word was sent over then to the country of the Danes that this killing had been done, and the Danes swore that they would have revenge. They got together a strong army and a fleet of ships, and came to Ireland and landed at a place named Clontarf, near Dublin. The Irish heard that they were coming, so they put together a large army and were ready for the Danes. The Irish had a fine leader called Brian Boru. When the Danes landed, Brian's army attacked them and drove them out again. They never came to take Ireland again, but a few came as visitors. I saw some of them myself, and they seemed all right to me!

When a foreign army like the Danes come in, it is hard to get rid of them all. I heard the old people say that the last Danes were living in Lettercath, away in the mountains. They were an old man and his son—the wife must have died. The poor old man wasn't interfering with anyone; he was as good a neighbour as anybody else. The Danes had a great name for making beer, and it was thought that they used the tips of the heather for it. The neighbours thought that it would be a good thing to find out how the beer was made—it might be better than the poteen they were making themselves, maybe! In any case, it wouldn't do the young people who drank it much harm.

Some men went to the old Dane to find out how he made the beer, and said that, if he wouldn't tell them, they would put himself and his son to death. The old man must have made a vow at one time that he would never tell the secret of the beer to anyone outside of his own country.

'Kill my son,' said he to the men, 'and then I'll tell ye how the beer is made!'

They tried to get the secret from him without killing the son, but it was no use. They killed the son.

'Kill myself now!' said the old man. 'I won't ever tell the secret to ye or to anybody else!'

I don't think that they killed the old man, but he lived only a short while after the death of his son. He was afraid that, if the son lived longer than himself, the Irish would force him to give up the secret, and he preferred the death of both of them to that happening. So from that day to this, the Irish never found out how the beer was made from the tips of the heather.

I heard the old people say that, whenever a young couple got married in the land of the Danes, their people would give them an acre of Irish land as a present. During the short time they spent in Ireland, they must have taken possession of a great deal of land. They had to leave it all behind them in a hurry at last. That broke their hearts, and though 'tis a long time since they left Ireland, they still think that they own the land here. It is said too that they hid a lot of wealth under the earth here, but it is hard to find it. I remember, when we used to be digging the ground in spring, the soil used to be full of small clay pipes; Danes' pipes we used to call them. They weren't anything as big as the pipes that are used now.

26 Cromwell and O'Donnell

THE HATRED WHICH CROMWELL'S ruthless deeds in Ireland in 1649-50 aroused in the hearts of the Irish people is reflected in this and other tales from oral tradition. The prophet (sometimes named Mac Amhlaoimh), who foretells the future for Cromwell and others, figures in other versions of this tale also. Some versions tell that Cromwell died in Ireland, that the Irish soil refused to receive his body, and that it drifted on the sea until it finally sank to the bottom of the Irish Sea, causing it to be very rough ever since!

There was a man here in Ireland long ago. He was a gentleman by the name of O'Donnell and he was very friendly with a monk in the district. One day the monk told him that there was a great change to come over Ireland; that England would take over Ireland, and that a leader of the name of Cromwell would be throwing the Irish people, who had land, out on the road and would be settling his own people from England in their place.

'The best plan for you,' said the monk to O'Donnell, 'is to go off over to England. The man they call Cromwell is a cobbler. You must travel around England, with a notebook, and ask every man you meet to sign his name in the book, promising that he won't ever take your land or dwelling-place off you. Keep on travelling like that until you go to where Cromwell is living.'

That was that! O'Donnell crossed over to England and he was travelling around with his book, pretending to be a bit simple, asking everyone he met to sign his book that he would never take his land or dwelling-place off him. He kept going till he came to Cromwell's house. He went in and asked Cromwell to put a side-patch on one of his shoes. When the job was done, he handed a guinea to Cromwell.

'A thousand thanks to you! That's good payment,' said Cromwell.

'Now,' said O'Donnell, 'I hope that you will sign this book that you will never take my land or dwelling-place off me.'

'Why wouldn't I promise you that?' said Cromwell.

He took hold of the book and signed in it that he would never take his land or dwelling-place off O'Donnell in Ireland. When he had done that, O'Donnell went back to Ireland.

Some years later, there was a great change in England. Cromwell rose up high and took the power from the king. Then he came to Ireland. He was throwing the people out of their land, whether they were noble or lowly, and killing them. He arrived at O'Donnell's house and struck a blow on the door.

'Out with you from here!' he shouted. 'You're here long enough!'

'I hope you won't put me out until you and myself have dinner together,' said O'Donnell.

'What sort of dinner have you?' asked Cromwell.

'Roast duck,' said O'Donnell.

'That's very good,' said Cromwell. 'I like that.'

Cromwell went into the house and the two of them started eating the dinner. When they had it eaten, O'Donnell took out his book and showed it to Cromwell.

'Do you recognise that writing?' said O'Donnell.

'I do, 'tis mine,' said Cromwell. 'How did you know that I'd be coming to Ireland or that I'd rise so high?'

It was no use for O'Donnell to hide it; he had to tell the truth to Cromwell.

'There was a holy monk in this place,' said he, 'and it was he that told me that a great change would come in Ireland and that it was a cobbler in England by the name of Cromwell who would come here and put me out of my land.'

'You must send for that holy monk for me,' said Cromwell, 'and if he doesn't come, I'll cut the head off him!'

O'Donnell went off and found the monk and brought him back to Cromwell.

'How did you get this knowledge?' asked Cromwell.

'I got it from Heaven,' replied the monk.

'Now you must tell me how long I will live,' said Cromwell.

'You will live as long as you wish to,' said the holy monk.

'I'll live for ever then!' said Cromwell.

There was another big gentleman from England along with Cromwell.

'And how long will I live? Will I get a long life?' he asked.

'If you pass the door of the next forge you meet on the road alive,' said the monk, 'you'll live a long time.'

'Ah, I'll live for ever so!' said the gentleman.

That was that! Cromwell didn't evict O'Donnell; he left him where he was, and went away. Himself and the English gentleman and their troop of soldiers went along, and when they were passing by a forge, Cromwell said:

'There's a shoe loose on one of our horses. But luckily we're near this forge!'

He jumped off his horse and entered the forge. The smith was inside.

'Hurry up and put a shoe on this horse for us!' said Cromwell.

The poor smith was trembling with terror. He hurried here and there about the forge, looking for a good piece of iron. He was afraid that he wouldn't be able to get a piece good enough for Cromwell and his army. Cromwell himself was searching around also, and he spied an old gun-barrel stuck above one of the rafters of the forge.

'Here's a piece of iron that's good!' said he.

He pulled down the old gun and shoved the barrel of it into the fire—he was well used to working in forges too, for his father was a smith. He started to blow the bellows. The English gentleman was standing outside the door. It wasn't long till the shot went off through the mouth of the gun and it struck the gentleman on his vest pocket and went out through his body at the other side. It killed him. Cromwell ran out when he heard the noise outside, jumped up on his horse, dug the spurs into it and raced for Dublin. As he was galloping along the road, whom did he see, walking ahead of him, but the holy monk! When the monk saw Cromwell coming towards him, he tried to run down and hide himself under the arch of a bridge.

'Come up out of that, you devil!' shouted Cromwell. 'If I have to go down to you, I'll cut the head off you!'

The monk came up to him.

' 'Tisn't from you I was hiding at all,' said the monk, ' but from the man behind you.'

' What man is behind me?' asked Cromwell.

' He's sitting behind you on the horse,' said the monk.

Cromwell looked behind him and he saw the Devil at his back. All he did was dig his spurs into his horse and race for Dublin. He went back to England and never returned to Ireland again. After spending a while in England, he grew restless. The King of Spain died, and his son, who hadn't much sense or knowledge about ruling a country, took his place. Cromwell decided on a plan which seemed very good to him. He wrote a letter to the young Spanish king, inviting him to England and offered him his daughter in marriage. When the king got the letter, he sent for his advisers and told them about it.

' That's a plan of Cromwell's,' said they, ' to try to get into this country and take over the kingdom. Write a letter back to him and say that you'd like such a marriage arrangement, but you want a year to think the matter over; when the year is out, you might like the offer very much. You must be strengthening your army during the year, and at the end of it, write to him and say that you don't wish to marry the Devil's daughter!'

Cromwell happened to be shaving himself when he got the letter at the end of the year. He had one side of his face shaved, when the letter was handed to him. When he read the piece about the Devil's daughter, he cut his throat with the razor and fell dead.

About the time when Cromwell killed himself, a ship was entering Liverpool, and the captain saw, coming towards him in the air, a fiery coach drawn by dogs, and they crying out: ' Clear the way for Oliver Cromwell!'

The Twining Branches (see page 83)

V Folk Prayers

THE PRAYERS IN THIS SECTION ARE taken from a collection entitled *Paidreacha na nDaoine*, edited by Searloit Ní Dhéisigh. A translation of the book into English was published under the title, *Prayers of the Gael*. Many such popular prayers have appeared in Douglas Hyde's *Abhráin Diadha Chúige Connacht* (The Religious Songs of Connacht), no date, as well as in *Knock Shrine Annual*, under the title, Guidhmís (Let us pray), contributed by Rev. Father Benedict, ODC, Dublin. Piaras de Hindeberg, now a Jesuit priest in Dublin, won his Master's Degree at University College, Dublin, some years ago by writing a thesis on such popular traditional prayers. It has not been published.

Occasional popular prayers, like the few given here, were very numerous in both Ireland and Scotland on the lips of speakers of the native language. They were quite distinct from the official prayers of the Church, and have great beauty and religious feeling. Practically every activity during the day was preceded by a particular prayer composed, possibly in the Middle Ages, for the purpose, and they were transmitted orally to succeeding generations.

For Scotland, Alexander Carmichael's *Carmina Gadelica*, with translations, gives an idea of their variety and richness.

Morning prayer when rising:

> I rise up with God.
> May God rise up with me!
> God's arm around me,
> While sitting or lying or rising. Amen.

Prayer said when entering a church:

> I salute you, O church of God!
> And may you salute me,
> In the hope that the twelve apostles
> May be praying for me today.
> I bow my right knee to the High King
> And my left knee to the Holy Spirit,
> In the hope that I may raise
> All before and behind me
> From Purgatory.

Prayer said when leaving a church:

> Goodbye, O house of God!
> The blessing of God about us!
> May the grace of God not leave us
> Until we return to His church!

Prayer before meals:

> Like the goodness of the five loaves and two fishes,
> Which God divided among the five thousand men,
> May the blessing of the King who so divided
> Be upon our share of this common meal!

Prayer after meals:

> A thousand thanks to You, O God,
> Who has given us this food for our bodies!
> May You give us everlasting food for our souls. Amen.

Prayer when milking:

> Come, Mary, and milk my cow!
> Come, St. Brigid, and protect her!
> Come, gentle St. Colmcille,
> And place your arm around my cow! Amen.

Prayer said when passing a graveyard:

> I salute ye, O faithful of Christ, who are here
> awaiting a glorious resurrection! May He who suffered
> the Passion for your sake grant you eternal rest! Amen.

Prayer said when raking the turf-fire at night:

> I cover over this fire
> As noble Christ did;
> Mary on top of the house,
> And St. Brigid in its centre.
> The eight strongest angels
> In the City of Graces,
> Guarding this house and hearth
> And bringing its people safe!

Prayer of fishermen:

> May the good luck of John and Peter
> Be on our nets! Amen.

Prayer before a journey:

> In the name of the victorious Father,
> In the name of the Son who suffered pain,
> In the name of the powerful Holy Spirit,
> May Mary and her Son be with us on our journey!

Prayer of a beggar-man:

> May the eternal Father give ye a share of the
> everlasting glory, and health to those who
> labour, and may God bring ye safe from any
> danger that may come upon ye!

VI Popular Charms

IN FORMER TIMES WHEN MEDICAL knowledge and expertise were at a low ebb, people had to depend on their own resources for the easement or curing of their ailments. In most districts there were one or two persons known locally as 'doctors', who were regarded as having special knowledge and curative powers. The manner in which they were said to have acquired these varied: such individuals as a seventh son or daughter in succession, a posthumous child, a person with a certain surname (Cahill or Keogh, to stop ringworm) or a person who was thought to be an associate of the fairies, and several others were supposed to have curative powers. People also made wide use of herbs and other things for medical purposes.

Besides the foregoing remedies to which persons had recourse in illness, they also depended on those (rather rare) individuals who could recite charms (a kind of apocryphal prayers) to cure particular ailments. There were hundreds of such charms (known in Irish as *orthaí*, Latin *orationes*) a few of which are given here.

There were, of course, many other charms apart from medical ones.

One day the holy Saviour, at the age of nine, and his mother were travelling along the road. They had come a long way, and neither a house nor farm was to be seen anywhere. At last they came in sight of a fine farm-house, towards dusk. They made their way to the door and the Virgin Mother asked for a night's lodging till morning. The woman of the house happened to be a strapping, strong, hard-hearted person. 'I have no suitable place for poor people,' said she. 'I'm sick and tired of beggars like ye!'

The Virgin said nothing but turned away from the door. They hurried along the road and had gone about forty spade-lengths, when they saw a man, who had a spade on his shoulder, jumping out over the fence near them. They saluted one another quietly.

'Poor woman,' said he, 'why didn't you stay in the house back there and rest for the night?'

'I wanted to stay there, my good man,' said the Virgin, 'but the woman of the house had no room for us.'

'No room in my house!' said the man. 'There's plenty of room for more than the two of you, good woman,' said he. 'I have a fine, roomy house. Turn back along with me and stay till morning!'

The Virgin and the boy followed him to the house. When his wife saw him coming with the pair whom she had turned away just before that, an angry look came on her face. She started to scold him, and the like of her abuse and blame was never before heard for having brought them back to the house!

'Take a seat up there, poor woman!' said the man of the house to the Virgin.

He showed herself and the boy to a seat by the fire. They were badly in need of a rest.

'See if you can get something to eat for the boy,' said the man to his wife. 'He has come a long journey, and boys are always hungry. Give him something to eat now, as supper won't be ready for a good while yet.'

'Get food for him yourself, if you think he's so hungry!' said his wife.

The man said no more, but turned down towards a small cupboard and got some milk and a thick slice of wheaten bread. He offered them to the boy. 'Be chewing that bread, little boy, until the supper is cooked,' said he.

The boy ate the bread and drank the milk until he was satisfied.

But nothing would pacify the woman of the house; she struck a blow at the pig and at the dog and at the cat, and kept up her bad temper until it was bed-time. When it was time to go to bed, the man spoke to his wife:

'Look around,' said he, 'and see if you can find something that the poor woman and her boy can lie on in the corner.'

'Look for it yourself—you're better able to do it than I am!' said his wife.

She walked off down to the room and went to bed for herself, leaving the man of the house trying to make a bed for the poor woman. He stood on a chair and reached into the loft where coarse flax-tow was thrown in a heap. He pulled down an armful of it and made a bed of it in the corner.

'Make the best you can of that, poor woman,' said he. 'At least 'tis better than the hard floor!'

He went off down to bed then and left them in the corner. It was when he had gone to bed that his wife really started to abuse the man; she scolded and persecuted him, so that anyone who could hear her would have pity for him. Her abuse went through the heart of the Virgin, who saw that she was the cause of it all.

'Son of my heart,' said she, 'isn't that good man a great pity, being scalded by that bad wife of his? Is there any way of controlling her?'

'No, mother,' said the boy. 'A rough, ill-tempered woman has never yet been controlled. The only thing to do is to take her husband from her.'

'I wouldn't like that to happen,' said the Virgin.

''Tis the only thing that will quieten her,' said the boy.

At that moment a sudden stitch of pain ran through the heart of the man of the house. He started to scream and screamed and screamed and, faith, when his wife heard the screams and the pitiful cries of pain from her husband, her abuse stopped and she jumped out of bed. She had something else to occupy her mind besides reviling and scolding him! She didn't know what to do.

'What ails you?' she asked him.

'I'm dying!' said he. 'I've a stitch in my heart!'

His wife didn't know where to find anyone to go to bring a priest or a doctor to him. His cries and screams were piercing the heart of the Virgin in the other room.

'Son of my heart,' said she, 'isn't it a pity that such a good man should die so soon. He's suffering terribly, and I'm sorry for him.'

'Do what you think best, mother,' said the Saviour, 'and I'll help you.'

The Virgin sat up on the edge of her bed of flax-tow, and pulled some wisps of it from under her son. She rolled them up and went to the bed of the sick man, pushed the tow under his side and laid her palm against it, saying:

> 'The gentle husband of a rude wife
> Put Jesus Christ lying on flax-tow;
> The palm of Mary on the stitch,
> In the Name of the Father, Son and Holy Spirit.'

No sooner had she said this than the pain of the stitch in the man's heart ceased, and before long he was better.

From that day to this, people have been curing a stitch with that charm. When anybody gets a severe stitch, old women set the charm, and it is said to cure it, by the grace of God.

Charm against the nightmare:

> Anne, the mother of Mary,
> Mary, the mother of Christ,
> Elizabeth, the mother of John the Baptist;
> I place those three between me and the bed-disease
> From tonight till a year from tonight
> And tonight as well.
> I go under your protection,
> O Tree on which Christ was crucified,
> To keep me from the nightmare,
> In the name of the Father and of the Son and of the Holy Spirit. Amen.

Charm against toothache:

> A charm set by Mary for her Son,
> In the doorway of Christ's City,
> Against pain and headache;
> May Jesus Christ banish from us
> The worm in the flesh,
> Which is harming the tooth,
> And kill it!
>   (followed by a Pater Noster, Ave Maria and Creed).

Charm against infection:

> I salute you, O green-leafed Tree,
> I salute you, O four-armed Cross,
> May no harm from this body before me
> Affect me, in the name of the Father
> and of the Son and of the Holy Spirit.
> Amen.
>
> —recited when going to the wake
> of someone who has died.

Charm against king's evil and eczema:

> In the name of Mary and of Saint Patrick, archbishop
> of all of Ireland, may every evil be banished
> from everywhere, in the name of the Father and of
> the Son and of the Holy Spirit. Amen
> (followed by a Pater Noster, Ave Maria,
> Gloria and Creed).

Charm to cure a sick cow:

> We set this charm for you, in the name of the
> Father and of the Son and of the Holy Spirit.
> Amen. This charm for you, O cow, from the
> manger of the Virgin in which Christ was born.
> 'Look, Mother! The cow is dying!' 'Look yourself,
> Son; You have the power.' 'Shake yourself,
> O cow, at my Mother's request, and give her
> thanks!' In the name of the Father and of the Son
> and of the Holy Spirit. Amen.

Seoirse de Barra and the Water-horse (see page 113)

VII Proverbs (Threes and Fours)

A PROVERB MAY BE DEFINED AS A homely truth of a general kind, expressed in a concise manner so as to recommend itself to a more or less extended circle. It has been described as 'the wisdom of many encapsuled by the wit of one'. Proverbs are, as a type of popular sayings, very ancient. They are not a mass product; each originated through one person, generally anonymous. As in most forms of folk literature, there has been constant borrowing between oral and literary sources in the case of proverbs.

Some proverbs use the devices of rhyme or alliteration to make them more easily remembered.

Instead of listing some ordinary Irish proverbs in translation here, I have selected some triads and a few 'fours', which were very numerous in the Irish language. Many of them have a rural flavour.

Proverbs (Threes and Fours)

The three best things:

>a little seed in good soil,
>a few cows in good grass,
>a few friends in the tavern.

The three hardest to teach:

>a woman, a pig and a mule.

The three keenest eyes:

>a hen's eye after a grain,
>a smith's eye after a nail,
>a young girl's eye at a fair.

The three most easily hurt:

>the eye, the elbow and the knee.

The three best friends and worst enemies:

>fire, wind and water.

The sharpest three:

>a thorn in a puddle, a fool's word and a flea.

The three who will reach Heaven most easily:

>a child after baptism,
>a priest after ordination,
>a poor farm-labourer.

The three most spirited:

>a widow's son who has cattle,
>a miller's dog which has meal,
>an old mare's foal which has grass.

The three best night's sleep of the farmer:

>the night after his crops have been sown,
>the night when he has his harvest in the barn,
>the night after he has paid his rent.

Three blows that keep a country prosperous:
>> the blow of an axe on wood,
>> the blow of a sledge on an anvil,
>> the blow of a flail on a threshing-floor.

Three things that never rest:
>> a waterfall,
>> the wind on the hillside,
>> a king otter.

The three hardest kinds of work:
>> reaping corn with a hook (sickle).
>> rowing in a storm,
>> sledging.

The three most difficult to choose:
>> a woman,
>> a razor,
>> a horse.

The fastest three in the sea:
>> a rayfish,
>> a seal,
>> a mackerel.

The three worst excesses:
>> too much seed in rich soil,
>> too many landlords in a country,
>> too many daughters in one house.

Three things to be avoided:
>> a beautiful wife,
>> a white cow,
>> a house on a high site.

The three strongest things:
>> fire,
>> water,
>> an enemy.

The hare's three gifts:

> power to turn swiftly,
> power to jump high,
> power to run speedily against a hill.

Three things that are as good as better things:

> dirty water to quench a fire,
> a blind man's ugly wife,
> a bad suit of clothes on a drunkard.

Three kinds of women whom a man cannot understand:

> a young woman,
> a middle-aged woman,
> an old woman.

The three most certain things:

> the rising and setting of the sun, and death.

The three liveliest:

> a young kitten.
> a kid,
> a young widow.

The three coldest things:

> a person's knee,
> a dog's nose,
> a water-drop from a cliff.

Three things which Christ forbade:

> the whistle of a woman,
> the barking of a hound,
> the crowing of a hen.

Three things which come silently:

> the rent day,
> old age.
> a beard.

The three best things a poor man can have:

> a mare,
> a sow,
> a goose.

The three most musical sounds:

> churning,
> ploughing,
> grinding corn.

Three things which Aristotle could not understand:

> the work of the bees,
> a woman's mind,
> the ebb and flow of the tide.

The three most beautiful sights:

> a potato-garden in bloom,
> a ship in sail,
> a woman after the birth of her child.

Three things that do not last:

> a maiden's love,
> a mare's love for her foal,
> the warmth of oaten bread.

Four profitless actions:

> Lighting a fire on a lake,
> Throwing stones at a wave,
> Advising a headstrong woman,
> Hammering cold iron.

The four worst things:

> A sore head,
> A bitter tongue,
> A troubled mind,
> An empty pocket.

The four things that best suit a thresher:

> A flail-handle of holly,
> A striking-stick of hazel,
> A single sheaf,
> A clean floor.

Four last ends:

> The end of a ship—sinking;
> The end of a kiln—burning;
> The end of feasting—dispraising;
> The end of laughing—sighing.

VIII Riddles

The following small selection from the scores of thousands of riddles found in both Irish and English in Ireland will serve to bring the prose texts in this volume to a close.

Metaphors such as riddles may well be the oldest form of oral lore, as they are the result of primary mental processes of association, comparison and the perception of similarities and differences. It is evident that they had an educational function side by side with being a means of amusement—the oldest riddles on record are found in school texts from Babylon. The phenomena of Nature and of life itself, have formed the varied base for both popular and literary riddles throughout the ages.

What is a herring worth when half-eaten?
—it is worth turning!

What goes up the water and down the water without reaching the top of the water?
—a mill-wheel.

What goes around the house and stops at the door?
> —the wall.

Why does a dog carry a bone in his mouth?
> —because he has no pocket.

It is outside,
It is inside,
It is in the corner,
With two hundred eyes.
> —a meal-sieve.

Buried was I before I died,
My grave lived and moved, and so did I.
> —Jonah in the whale's belly.

What is brought to the table, is always cut but never eaten?
> —a deck of cards.

An old red cow lying by the wall,
Eats all she gets and drinks none at all.
> —a fire.

I have a little calf and she eats all before her;
If she drank anything, she'd die.
> —a fire.

The more you take, the more you leave behind.
> —footsteps.

'Tis in the corner, it never leaves the corner, and yet it travels the whole world.
> —a stamp on a letter.

I have a little Kerry cow,
She is as good as any cow,
She sits in the corner with one horn.
> —a kettle.

'Tis red in the bottom, black in the middle and white on top.
> —A cake of bread on a griddle over a fire.

The Foot of Rooska Hill (see page 159)

IX Songs and Ballads

SONGS OF VARIOUS KINDS IN THE Irish language number scores of thousands. While many of them have been collected and published, countless numbers of them must have been lost without ever having been recorded in any way. Many are still alive and are sung, of course, when a suitable occasion offers.

When the English language began to spread in Ireland some hundreds of years ago, the practice arose of translating Irish songs into English, and so there came about what are known as macaronic songs, with alternate verses in Irish and in English.

In the following selection some samples are given of songs which were composed and sung in English. Like most songs and ballads, the authors are generally anonymous. The themes were as varied as human life itself.

27 The Maid of Magheracloone

THIS SONG ABOUT AN UNHAPPY love affair was very popular some years ago in the south-eastern part of County Monaghan. The district concerned is in the barony of Farney, close to the borders of Counties Meath and Louth. According to local tradition, the disappointed 'maid' was said to have been named Carroll, and the lover who deserted her was named McCabe.

Ye maidens all, both great and small, come listen unto me,
Till I relate my doleful state and my sad destiny.
I was courted by a comely lad, but ah, he left me soon
A broken-hearted maiden on the hills of Magheracloone.

Many a pleasant evening beneath the hawthorn tree
I listened to his merry jokes of innocence and glee;
But now, alas! Those flattering words have almost proved my ruin,
And left me here to mourn on the hills of Magheracloone.

Many a lonely night I spend behind the window blind;
I think I hear his footsteps come when, ah, 'tis but the wind;
Or the rustling of the fallen leaves along the pavement strewn,
Reminding me when he'd call to see the maid of Magheracloone.

He cares not for to meet me now on a Sunday after Mass;
He cares not for to watch my steps as homeward I do pass.
Going home from his night's rambles, I can hear his merry tune,
Going whistling by the lonely home of the maid of Magheracloone.

I blame him not. The fault is mine, I really must confess,
For I heeded not his merry jokes, his smiles or fond caress.
To another lad I gave my love both morning, night and noon,
Which banished him far, far away from the hills of Magheracloone.

The Winter now is past and gone and Spring is drawing near,
And with it too my heart has grown both fervent and sincere.
Where is the hand that used to pluck the flowers in full bloom,
And weave them in the silken curls of the maid of Magheracloone?

But he never will return again to view the sylvan shades;
No more I'll hear those flattering words which first my heart betrayed;
No more he'll meet his darling by the lamplight or the moon
Or press within his loving arms the maid of Magheracloone.

The cruel chains of torment cling fast around my breast;
Here on my bed of thorns I seek my troubled rest.
So you now must only pity me and think on the sad doom
Of a broken-hearted maiden on the hills of Magheracloone.

28 Down by Mount Callan's Side

THE FOLLOWING RATHER HUMOROUS ballad describes how a young man was 'cured' of his thirst and love-sickness by a drink of milk given to him by a milk-maid, and how marriage swiftly followed the inspection of his landed property by the girl's father.

Mount Callan (Sliabh Colláin) is a hill, over 1280 feet in height, in the parish of Inagh in West Clare. 'The Hand' is a cross-roads, and Doolough (Black Lake) lies in the adjoining parish of Kilmurry.

One evening fair as I roved out, being troubled in my mind,
To view the groves and valleys fair and the meadows in their prime,
Approaching the Hand, I met a lass, who has my heart beguiled,
And she milking of her father's cow, down by Mount Callan's side.

I instantly saluted her and put her in a maze;
I asked her would she quench my thirst, as the milk was in her pail.
She says: 'Young man, I pray, be gone! I hope you won't me chide,
For I'm milking of my father's cow, down by Mount Callan's side.

'What matter if you give a drink. You know it won't be missed,
For I am much in want of it; I hope you won't resist.
Here in pain I must remain, if you do not divide,
For Cupid's dart has pierced my heart down by Mount Callan's side.'

'If milk be all the cure you want, I'll heal you of your pain;
But as you've been as bad as that, I fear it's all in vain.
Come drink enough and quench your thirst, in hopes you may survive,
And do not blame a simple dame for the losing of your life.'

The milk being filled, I took a drink and found it very mild;
I drank a health to my true love and wished she would be mine.
She says: 'Young man, it's all a plan, how soon you want a wife,
And you as bad so late as that, down by Mount Callan's side.'

'If I had been as bad as that a little while ago,
But now you have improved my health and eased me of my woe.
The doctor that prescribed the cure, it's right she should be mine,
To wed in peace on my estate for the saving of my life.'

'Kind sir, your offer, it is good. I'm sure you're very kind,
But what of your prosperity, or where do you reside?
My father is a wealthy man, by him I must abide,
For he reared me up most tenderly, down by Mount Callan's side.'

Says I: 'My lass, your good remarks are very shrewd and wise.
My estate is by Lough Doolough Lake, and I'm an only child.
Through rural plains and fertile vales, your carriage you can drive,
And bless the day you cured the swain, down by Mount Callan's side.'

I went straight to her father and showed him all my deeds
And asked him to come with me, till my estate he'd see.
He seemed to be quite satisfied and got us wed that night,
Five hundred pounds he counted out, down by Lough Doolough's side.

Then the carriage was got ready, and we drove to sweet Kinsale;
The joy-bells, they were ringing, and the bands did sweetly play.
Let all fair maids be mild and chaste and look to my advice,
And give a drink to a swain that's ill, down by Mount Callan's side.

29 The Foot of Rooska Hill

IT IS TO BE HOPED THAT SUCH fickle lasses as the one mentioned in this song do not exist in real life!

One day for recreation, quite easy in my mind,
The fields all round were brightly crowned with flowers of every kind,
About mid-day I chanced to stray down by a rippling rill;
As I did pass, I met a lass at the foot of Rooska Hill.

She was not vain, but neat and plain, and she was not too tall;
I own she wore a purple robe, likewise a knitted shawl;
Her golden hair was flowing fair; in her voice there was a thrill;
I really thought she was a queen that stood on Rooska Hill.

I was amazed. On her I gazed, as she stood in my view;
My heart did beat, so fast and fleet, I thought 'twould break in two;
I then arose and did propose, and that with right good will,
Saying: 'Come with me, my dearest dear, tonight from Rooska Hill'.

She said: 'Young man, you're speaking wrong. I cannot grant your request;
I'm waiting here for my Willie dear, he's the lad that I love best;
I'll meet him yet about sunset down by that purling rill,
And we both will rove along the grove at the foot of Rooska Hill'.

I said again: 'There are good men perhaps that you don't know.'
'Oh, that may be, indeed,' says she, 'but there's none like Willie O.
So go your way without delay; you cannot change me still,
For I'll live and die with my darling boy at the foot of Rooska Hill.'

'Oh, maiden dear, now pity me, for I have a broken heart;
'Twill be my doom to face the tomb, if from you I must part.
If you're inclined to prove unkind, myself I'll surely kill,
And my corpse quite cold you will behold tonight on Rooska Hill.'

With a heavy sigh, she then drew nigh and took me by the hand,
Saying: 'Come with me, my dearest dear, we'll join in wedlock bands;
I'll be your wife for future life, let it be for good or ill;
And we'll bless the day we came this way to the foot of Rooska Hill.'

30 Famous Kildorrery Town

THE FIRST TIME THAT I HEARD THIS SONG was a night in the early Spring of 1921 when I was a passenger on a train not far from the town named in the title of the song. The carriage was crowded with British soldiers, and the singer, the only other civilian except myself, was a young man of about twenty-five. The soldiers seemed to like the lively tune, as I did, and hummed the chorus at the end of each verse.

This song is in the style of 'Famous Dromcolliher Town' (not far away) composed by Percy French.

I've been to Crosshaven and Youghal,
Ballybunion, Tramore and Kilkee,
Ballycotton and likewise Dungarvan,
Those famous resorts by the sea,
For my health I've been travelling through Ireland,
But now I'm at last settled down,
Though lacking in wealth, I've been gaining my health,
Since I came to Kildorrery Town.

Chorus
I suppose you all know of Kildorrery;
If you don't, well, indeed, that is queer;
Sure, 'tis only five miles from Ardpatrick
And three from the Cross of Redchair.
And when at that cross you are landed,
You will see a big hill looking down,
And on top of that hill, looking naked and chill,
Lies famous Kildorrery Town.

When King Edward came over to Ireland
In delicate health, as you know,
I met him one day in my travels,
And he asked me which way he would go.
Says he: ' 'Tis fresh air I am seeking,
As my system is badly run down.'
' Oh, King Edward,' says I, ' the best air you can try
Is up in Kildorrery Town.'

Chorus

When the pilgrims went over from Ireland
To visit the people of Rome,
'Twas little they thought the surprises
That city had for them in store.
They went to the Pope at his palace,
And when he had seated them down,
In a voice loud and clear, says he: ' Is anyone here
From famous Kildorrery Town?'

Chorus

When Saint Patrick—he lived up in Ulster—
To the South he thought he'd come down,
And where do you think he sought lodgings,
But up in Kildorrery Town?
But when on the road from Kilmallock,
At Ardpatrick he died on the way,
Those who stood by his side on the day that he died
Could hear him distinctly to say:

' Oh, I'll never get up to Kildorrery,
Though much I have longed to be there;
Sure, 'tis only five miles from Ardpatrick
And three from the Cross of Redchair.
Make my grave on the hill of Ardpatrick,
And there let my bones be laid down;
But my soul, when I die, ere it reaches the sky,
Will visit Kildorrery Town!

Chorus

31 The Alfred de Snow

DISASTERS AT SEA ARE A RECURRING theme in balladry. The tragedy in each case is described in simple language, but a certain amount of exaggeration is, nevertheless, to be expected.

In the following instance, the ship was lost in a storm near the mouth of Waterford Harbour, where the rivers Suir and Barrow enter the sea.

Some manuscript versions of the ballad give the name of the ship as 'The Alfred D. Snow'.

Of shipwrecks and disasters we've read and seen a deal
Out off the coast of Wexford, to tell a dreadful tale;
It being on the fourth of January, when a winding gale did blow,
And nine and twenty lives were lost on board the *Alfred de Snow*.

Kind friends, I say attention pay, I won't detain you long,
While I will unfold the mournful facts of this most feeling song;
My humble pen can scarce begin these verses for to write;
There's no poet's brain can e'er explain the horrors of that night.

That unlucky day she sailed away to plough the stormy foam;
To say there's not one soul alive to bring the tidings home;
The night before our ship was lost, 'twas mournful for to tell,
She was like a feather in the wind, tossed up on every swell.

From the port of San Francisco she sailed across the main,
Bound for the port of Liverpool, her cargo it was grain.
She tried to make the harbour, but in shelter of the land
That good ship went in fragments next morning on the strand.

Are there any hearts of sympathy now standing on our shore?
Oh, yes, there's brave and gallant men, now watching in Dunmore;
They're ready for to risk their lives; to the coastguard's house they go;
They asked the captain for the boat, but he quickly told them 'No!'

At last, I'm told, he gave consent to this noble-hearted crew,
And in spite of storm, tide and rain, to the sinking ship they flew;
But as they reached the sinking ship, the crew in hopes to save,
They saw the last let go the mast and sink beneath the wave.

'Twas a sudden splash that broke her mast; her mainsail split in two;
Her yards were floating by her side; she's sinking from our view.
Oh, watch that small and fragile boat, now bumping by her side!
Oh heavens, there are human beings now floating in the tide!

'Twas the dauntless Captain Cotter, with his *Dauntless* ship by name,
With spirits brave, he faced the wave, to their assistance came.
It was like a thing that was to be, when close up by her side,
Her engines stopped, her paddles broke, she drifted with the tide.

You sank last night within our sight, in spite of all our skill;
Our ship today has broken away, 'neath the sandbanks of Broomhill;
There's only seven bodies got out of twenty-nine in all;
In consecrated clay, they lie today, to await Saint Michael's call.

Poor fellows, it was hard on them, just as their voyage was o'er,
After four long months and twenty days to perish on the shore.
May they take a trip in Our Saviour's ship along Jehovah's shore,
And join the other twenty-two and part from them no more!

32 Francie Hynes

THIS FINAL BALLAD HAS AS ITS THEME the hanging of a man who had been found guilty of murder. In a few such ballads, the condemned man may occasionally admit his implication in the crime. In many others, however, as in the following one, he may protest his innocence to the last.

You feeling christians, one and all,
I hope you'll pray for me;
I had to end my youthful life
At the age of twenty-three.

All for the crime of murder
I was condemned to die
On the eleventh of September
Upon the gallows high.

Now, Francie Hynes it is my name.
Good christians, for me pray.
I leave good, kind relations
To mourn me today.
In fact, all over Ireland,
With a sympathising eye,
Will drop a tear and breathe a prayer,
When they hear I have to die.

I never own I did this deed;
But, oh alas to say,
There is many a one as well as me,
Whose life they took away.
I'll put my trust and confidence
In Him whose blood did flow,
To get that mercy from my God
Which no earthly judge can show.

They say that I shot Doolarty;
But never have I done
A much less crime than to take a life.
I never rose the gun.
My name he only mentioned,
As he saw me to pass by;
This was the only evidence
Condemned me for to die.

Farewell, my loving brothers,
Likewise my sisters too,
When my soul is with my blessed Lord,
I'll intercede for you.
I know your hearts will break for me,
For I never did the crime,
But think on Our Saviour's blessed wounds
That was pierced the second time.

May God defend my chaplain,
Who did his duty well;
Both night and day for me did pray,
While in my prison cell.
On the day of my execution,
He stood there by my side,
Until the gallow's scaffold
Erected I did spy.

At last the fatal bolt was drawn;
His soul had passed away.
Above the ramparts of the jail,
A black flag did display
To show the soul of Francie Hynes
From all earthly clay did flee,
To live with God and Mary pure
For all eternity.

With pain I drop my feeble pen;
I have no more to say;
But for the soul of Francie Hynes
Let all good christians pray.
Unto his execution
He longingly did cry:
'Come, draw the bolt! I'm innocent
And reconciled to die.'

Notes

I MYTHOLOGICAL AND HERO TALES, pages 17–66

1 BALOR AND GAIBHDE THE SMITH
IFC Ms. Vol. 289 : 296-305. Recorded 19 October, 1936, by Aodh Ó Domhnaill from Sorcha, Bean Mhic Ghrianna (61), of Rannafast, County Donegal, who had heard it from her mother, aged 92, of the same district.

International tales inset into this story include Type 934C* Man will Die if ever he Sees his Daughter's Son and Type 1137 The Ogre Blinded : Polyphemus.

Motifs include D1652.3.1 (Cow with inexhausible milk), H1141 and H1142 (Task: eating enormous amount, and drinking enormous amount), and D1004 (Magic tear). The motif of the origin of the crooked throw of women may be Irish. For the right of taking a bride on her wedding-night (*jus primae noctis*), see also the legend about the 'Danes' in this volume.

2 THE FATE OF THE SONS OF UISNEACH
IFC Vol. 850 : 121-33. Recorded July 30, 1942, by Liam Mac Coisdeala, full-time collector, from Éamonn a Búrc, Aill na Brón, Kilkerrin, Carna, County Galway. Éamonn, who died in November of that year, was one of the finest traditional storytellers in Ireland. The tale belongs to the Táin Bó Chuailgne (Cattle-raid of Cooley) cycle of Ulster storytelling, and the earliest manuscript mention of it dates from the ninth century. Its theme—the elopement of a young woman from her elderly suitor with a more youthful lover—became a part of the literary tradition of Europe, and is to be found in the stories of Tristan and Isolde and Diarmaid and Gráinne. John Millington Synge, the Irish playwright, used the tale as the basis for his play, *Deirdre of the Sorrows*. For a discussion of the story, see Bruford, *Gaelic Folktales and Medieval Romances* 99-104. A fairly usual ending to the tale (Aarne-Thompson Type 970 : The Twining Branches) is absent from the present version.

Motifs include D1840-D1847 Magic invulnerability; Z65.1 Red as blood, white as snow; N733.1 Brothers unwittingly fight each other; T575.1 Child speaks in mother's womb.

3 DIARMAID AND GRAINNE

IFC Ms. Vol. 1538 : 99-107. Recorded by Seán Ó Heochaidh, full-time collector, from Micí (Sheáin) Ó Baoill, Rannafast, County Donegal, in 1954.

The theme of the desertion of an aged suitor for a younger one, as Finn is here deserted by Gráinne for Diarmaid, has its parallels in the story of Deirdre and Naoise, and the present Irish tale is undoubtedly the source for the romance of Tristan and Iseult. It was very popular in the oral tradition of both Ireland and Scotland. It was mentioned as early as the tenth century in a saga-list, and the earliest full manuscript version of it dates from the fourteenth century.

Many dolmens throughout Ireland were popularly known as Leapacha Dhiarmada agus Ghráinne (Beds of Diarmaid and Gráinne) as a result of the flight of the lovers as described in the tale.

For discussions of the tale, see Alan Bruford, *Gaelic Folktales and Mediaeval Romances (Béaloideas, XXXIV)*, 106-109, 1966, and Gerard Murphy, *Duanaire Finn* (Irish Texts Society, XLIII), 1953.

Motifs include D1811.1.1 Thumb of knowledge; H900-H1399 Tests of prowess: tasks; J652 Inattention to warnings; T157 Fiancée forces elopement with another man.

4 FINN AND THE BIG MAN

IFC Ms. Vol. 983 : 72-89. Recorded by Ediphone about 1930 by Dr Robin Flower from Peig Sayers on the Blasket Islands in West Kerry, and transcribed in 1946 by Seosamh Ó Dálaigh, full-time collector for the Irish Folklore Commission. Flower recorded many tales and songs from Peig and others on the Great Blasket. Peig was one of the best women-storytellers in Ireland until her death in 1958; a monument was erected by friends and admirers over her grave in 1969.

The name of the 'Big Man' is given as Rí na bhFear nGorm (The King of the Black Men) in other versions of this tale, which faintly resembles Type 300 The Dragon-Slayer. The episode in which Finn hides in the cradle is an ecotype of Type 1149 Children Desire Ogre's Flesh, of which more than one hundred versions have been recorded in Ireland.

Finn may originally have been another name for the god, Lugh. Tales of the Fianna were very rare in manuscript tradition until the twelfth century, but became very popular in later centuries. Motifs include B11.10 Sacrifice of human being to dragon; D1840ff. Magic invulnerability; D1841.3 Burning magically evaded; D1841.5 Invulnerability from weapons; D1841.6 Immunity from drowning; D838.8 Magic helmet; F1071.2.1 Enormous leap; G308.1 Fight with sea/lake monster; H900-H1399 Tests of prowess; K1839.12 Disguise as child in cradle, and T585.5 Child born with all his teeth.

5 YOUTH, THE WORLD AND DEATH

IFC Ms. Vol. 1343: 434-41. Recorded by Seán Ó Heochaidh on Ediphone cylinders, 21 September, 1954, from Micí (Sheáin Néill) Ó Baoighill, Rannafast, County Donegal.

A large number of versions of this tale has been collected in Ireland. An early Irish version of it can be found in the frame-story, Feis Tighe Chonáin, edited by Nicholas O'Kearney, *Transactions of the Ossianic Society*, II (1854), 146-57, with English translation. A translation of a Kerry version of the tale can be found in *Folktales of Ireland*, edited by Sean O'Sullivan, University of Chicago Press and Routledge and Kegan Paul, London (1966), 57-60. Professor Carl W. von Sydow of Lund, Sweden, in an article entitled 'Tors Färd till Utgaard' (*Danske Studier*), 1910, pointed to probable affinities between a tale in Snorri Sturluson's Edda and Feis Tighe Chonáin. See also *The Bardic Stories of Ireland*, 132-35, Patrick Kennedy, 1886; and *The Vikings and the Viking Wars in Irish and Gaelic Tradition*, 30-2, Reidar Th Christiansen, Oslo, 1931.

Motifs include D2143.3 Fog produced by magic; D6 Enchanted castle; F771.6 Phantom house: disappears at dawn; K1886.2 Mists which lead astray; Z110 Personifications, and Z111 Death personified.

6 THE EVERLASTING FIGHT

IFC Ms Vol. 157: 197-211. Recorded on an Ediphone, September, 1935, by Liam Mac Coisteala, full-time collector, from Padhraic Mac an Iomaire, Coillín, Carna, County Galway, who had learned the story from his own grandfather fifty years previously. More than 200 versions of this tale have been recorded in Ireland.

Bruford (*Gaelic Folktales and Mediaeval Romances*, 220-1) states that the series of quests on which the hero is sent after slaying the hag is an Irish development, not found in Scottish versions. Many Irish versions end on a humorous note.

Motifs include B871.1.6 Giant cat; E102 Resuscitation by magic liquid; E155.1 Slain warriors revive nightly; H1200ff. Quests; K1863 Death feigned to learn how soldiers are resuscitated; P556 Challenge to battle.

7 CU THE SMITH'S SON

IFC Ms. Vol. 498: 127-43. Recorded in 1933 by Liam Mac Coisdeala, full-time collector, from Éamonn a Búrc, Aird Mhór, Carna, County Galway. Éamonn had learned the story from his father.

The tale contains several traits which belong to hero tales in the Irish storytelling tradition: *geasa* (magical injunctions), quests in search of the heroine and for the king's missing teeth, and 'runs' (rhetorics) descriptive of voyages, challenges, combats and the final end-'run'.

Motifs include B401 Helpful horse; D2143.3 Fog produced by magic; E783 Vital head: retains life after being cut off; H1200ff. Quests; N825.1 Childless old couple adopt hero; P556 Challenge to battle; Q241 Adultery punished; Q414 Punishment: burning alive; Q416 Punishment: drawing asunder by horses; R10.1 Princess/Maiden abducted; T640 Illegitimate children.

II ORDINARY FOLKTALES, pages 67–86

8 JUDAS
IFC Ms. Vol. 73 : 297-306. Recorded 19 January, 1932, by Mícheál Ó Flannagáin, teacher from Pádhraic Ó Maoláin, Eonacht, Aran Islands, County Galway.
Type 931 Oedipus.
Motifs include F730 Extraordinary islands; H1381.1 Quest for unknown parents; H51.1 Recognition by birthmark; M343 Parricide prophecy; M344 Mother-incest prophecy; Q560.2 Respite from Hell; R131 Exposed or abandoned child rescued, and V316 Efficacy of prayer.

It may also be apposite to mention two associated, though, somewhat conflicting, motifs: E489.7 Judas Iscariot appears in midst of sea on rock washed alternately by fiery and icy waves, and Q560.0.3 Soul of Judas tormented on rock in sea on certain days as respite from pains of hell. See *Catalogue of Manuscripts in the British Museum*, II, 544, Robin Flower, 1926; also *Lives of the Irish Saints*, II, 65, 96, Charles Plummer, 1922. See the entry under Judas Iscariot in Funk and Wagnalls *Standard Dictionary of Folklore, Mythology and Legend*, II, 560-1, New York, 1950.

9 THE BEST WAY TO GOD
IFC Ms. Vol. 983 : 90-100. Recorded on an Ediphone in the 1930s by Dr Robin Flower from Peig Sayers of the Great Blasket Island, County Kerry. The recording was transcribed in 1946 by Seosamh Ó Dálaigh, full-time collector.

The tale seems to be related to Type 471 The Bridge to the Other World.

Motifs are F1 Journey to otherworld as dream or vision; V510ff. Visions, and Q286 Uncharitableness punished.

10 THE KING OF SUNDAY
IFC Ms. Vol. 76 : 130-45. Recorded for Seán Mac Giollarnáth, Galway, from Éamonn Ó Fíne, An Pháirc, An Spidéal, County Galway, 4 September, 1932.

This tale is a religious ecotype of Type 461 Three Hairs from the Devil's Beard, especially of sections III, IV and V of that tale. Its main theme is a journey to the Otherworld, as seen from the christian point of view. The application of the title 'King' to the Deity in connection with the days of the week is usual in Irish poetry and religious tales, e.g., the Irish name for Sunday is *Dia Domhnaigh* (the day of the Lord).

Motifs in this tale include H900 Tasks imposed; H1090 Tasks requiring miraculous speed; E755.3 Souls in purgatory; F171.1 Fat and lean kine in otherworld, and Q566 (Punishments by heat in hell).

11 THE DRY AND WET FUNERAL DAYS

IFC Ms. Vol. 1510: 21-9. Recorded on Ediphone cylinders in October, 1957, by Seán Ó Heochaidh, full-time collector, from Mící (Sheáin Néill) Ó Baoill, Rannafast, County Donegal.

This tale is an Irish ecotype of Type 461 Three Hairs from the Devil's Beard, the tale being mainly concentrated on sections III, IV and V of the international Type. Hundreds of versions of it have been recorded in Ireland.

The main motifs are: C283 Tabu: eating without giving thanks; H1291 Questions asked on way to other world; H1292.5 Question (on quest): How can the girl thus far avoided by suitors marry?; Q286 Uncharitableness punished.

Glendowan is in the parish of Gartan in County Donegal.

12 THE TWINING BRANCHES

IFC Ms. Vol. 911: 282-8. Recorded in December, 1943, by Seosamh Ó Dálaigh, full-time collector, from Peig Sayers, Great Blasket Island, County Kerry. She had heard this and all of her many stories from her father, who lived on the mainland nearby.

Aghadoe is near the town of Killarney in County Kerry. Almost a hundred versions of this tale have been recorded in Ireland.

Type 970; motif E631.0.1 Twining branches grow from graves of lovers.

III LEGENDS AND FOLK BELIEF, pages 87–127

13 FATED TO BE HANGED

IFC Ms. Vol. 146: 191-5. Recorded on Ediphone cylinders, 15 September, 1935, by Tadhg Ó Murchú, full-time collector, from Seán (Mhártain) Ó Súilleabháin, Emlaghmore, Iveragh, County Kerry.

This tale belongs to the genre known as Tales of Fate (Types 930-939).

Motifs included are M391.1 Fulfilment of prophecy successfully avoided and V222.1.1 Radiance fills church when saint dies.

14 THE MOUTHLESS CHILD
IFC Ms Vol. 1489: 119-21. Recorded on the Ediphone, July, 1956, by Seán Ó Heochaidh, full-time collector, from Séamus Mac Amhlaoigh (79), Na Saileasaí, parish of Inver, County Donegal. A similar story was recorded by Professor Kenneth H. Jackson from Peig Sayers of the Great Blasket Island, County Kerry, and was published by him in *Béaloideas* (Journal of the Folklore of Ireland Society), VIII (1938), p.60. Professor Jackson has further discussed this theme, and I have summarised and commented on related tales in articles to be published in that Journal, Volume XXXVII.

Motifs: C993 Unborn child affected by mother's broken tabu; F513.0.3 Mouthless People; L435.2 Self-righteous woman punished; Q221.6 Lack of trust in God punished; T551.6 Child born without mouth.

15 SAINT COLMCILLE AND TORY ISLAND
IFC Ms. Vol. 1141: 56-60. Recorded in July, 1942, by Tomás Mac Sabhaois, from Mící (Sheáin Néill) Ó Baoill, Rannafast, County Donegal.

Motif: V222.7 Dead holy man stretches hand from tomb to honour saint.

The saint's name is pronounced 'Colmkille'.

16 SEAN SLAMMON'S DREAM
IFC Ms. Vol. 181: 2-16. Recorded on 10 March 1936, by Liam Mac Coisdeala, full-time collector, from Seán Ó Cuinneagáin, Bunnadubber, Currandulla, County Galway.

The tale may be likened to that told about Daniel O'Rourke in Crofton Croker's *Fairy Legends of the South of Ireland* (1862), 140-8, and Alfred Perceval Graves' *The Irish Fairy Book* (1938), 25-35. In much the same vein are the hunting *(Fiadhach)* poems of Antoine Raftery, edited by Douglas Hyde.

The places mentioned in the tale are mainly in County Galway, but Clare, Sligo and even Scotland are also named.

Motif: F471.1 Nightmare.

17 THE FAIRY FROG
IFC Ms. Vol. 850: 165-73. Recorded 1 August, 1942, by Liam Mac Coisdeala, full-time collector, from Éamonn a Búrc, Aill na Brón, Kilkerrin, Co. Galway.

Notes 173

For further references to this widespread story, see *Folklore Fellows Communications*, No. 175 (1958), 'The Migratory Legends', No. 5070 (Midwife to the Fairies), by Reidar Th. Christiansen, in which a large number of Norwegian references is cited.

Motifs: F234.1.6 Fairy in form of frog; F379.2 Objects brought home from fairyland.

18 THE CAKES OF OATMEAL AND BLOOD
IFC Ms. Vol. 938: 127-35. Recorded on an Ediphone, March, 1944, by Seán Ó Cróinín, full-time collector, from Amhlaoimh Ó Loingse, Cúil Ao, County Cork.

Motifs: E0-E199 Resuscitation.

19 THE SPIRIT, THE SAILOR AND THE DEVIL
IFC Ms. Vol. 983: 250-58. Recorded in the 1930s by Dr Robin Flower from Peig Sayers on the Great Blasket Island off the west coast of Kerry. The tale was transcribed from Flower's Ediphone cylinders many years later by Seosamh Ó Dálaigh, full-time collector for the Irish Folklore Commission.

Motifs: D2141 Storm produced by magic; H932 Tasks assigned to the devil.

20 SEOIRSE DE BARRA AND THE WATER-HORSE
IFC Ms. Vol. 181: 516-26. Recorded on an Ediphone by Liam Mac Coisdeala, 14 April 1936, from Micheál Ó Coincheannain, Roinn na Háirne, Cor an Dola, County Galway.

The name of the hero in this tale is Seoirse de Barra (George Barry), and the place where the memorial monument *(leacht* or *carn)* was raised to him is now known as Lough George (Leacht Seoirse). It is situated about eight miles north-east of Galway City and about five miles from the eastern shore of Lough Corrib in County Galway.

Motifs: F420.1.3.3 Water-spirit as horse; F492 Death on horseback; F989.13 Animal dives into lake and disappears; Z72.1 A year and a day.

21 THE CONNEELYS AND THE SEALS
IFC Ms. Vol. 850: 256-63. Recorded 18 July, 1942, by Liam Mac Coisdeala, full-time collector, from Éamonn a Búrc, Aill na Brón, Kilkerrin, County Galway.

Motifs: B601.18 Marriage to seal; B631.2 Human beings descended from seals; D327.2 Seal becomes person.

David Thomson's book, *People of the Sea*, has many legends about seals and other sea-beings. See also No. 4080 in Reider Th.

Christiansen's 'The Types of the Migratory Legends' *(Folklore Fellows Communications)* (1958).

22 THE WOUNDED SEAL
IFC Ms. Vol. 983 : 374-81. Recorded on an Ediphone in the 1930s by Dr Robin Flower from Peig Sayers of the Great Blasket, County Kerry, and transcribed by Seosamh Ó Dálaigh, full-time collector, in 1947.
For motifs, see notes to the preceding story.

23 THE FORK AGAINST THE WAVE
IFC Ms. Vol. 386 : 170-6. Recorded on an Ediphone, 6 August, 1937, by Seosamh Ó Dálaigh, full-time collector, from Mícheál Mac Gearailt, Coumeenole, Dunquin, County Kerry.
Motifs : F420.1.2 Water-spirit as woman (water-nymph, water-nix); F420.5.2.1.1 Water-maiden enamours man and draws him under water.

24 THE SOUL AS A BUTTERFLY
IFC Ms. Vol. 859 : 107-111. Recorded in March, 1943, by Seosamh Ó Dálaigh, full-time collector, from Peig Sayers of the Blasket Islands. Peig had, since the previous year, been settled on the mainland at Ballinahow.
This is a version of the Guntram Legend, told about a so-named king of the Burgundians. The earliest version of the legend is in Paulus Diaconus' *Historia gentis Langobardorum,* written about 787. An English translation by W. D. Foulke was published in Philadelphia in 1807. For other references to, and versions of, the legend, see : The Migratory Legends, Reidar Th. Christiansen, No. 4000, pp. 57-58 *(Folklore Fellows Communications,* No. 175, Helsinki, 1958); 'Die Guntramsage : Type 1645A', Hannjost Lixfeld, *Fabula* 13/1972, 60-107; *Gesta Romanorum,* tale CLXXII, 1959; *Carmina Gadelica,* II, 361-2, Alexander Carmichael, Edinburgh (1928); *Celtic Folklore,* II, 601-4, J. Rhys, Oxford (1901); and for another Irish version from the Dingle Peninsula, from which area the present version came, see *Fiche Blian ag Fás* (Twenty Years A-Growing), by Maurice O'Sullivan, first edition (1933), 22—
The relevant motif is E734.1 Soul in form of butterfly.

IV HISTORICAL TRADITION, pages 129-135

25 THE 'DANES'
IFC Ms. Vol. 1489 : 502-8. Recorded in August, 1957, by Seán Ó

Heochaidh, full-time collector, from Micí (Sheáin Néill) Ó Baoill, Rannafast, County Donegal.

Motifs: J624 Uniting against a common enemy; N511 Treasure in ground; S63 Spouse murder pact; T161 Jus primae noctis.

See *The Vikings and the Viking Wars in Gaelic Tradition*, Reidar Th. Christiansen, Oslo, 1931. For the legend of the Danish heather-beer, see *The Types of the Irish Folktale*, Ó Súilleabháin and Christiansen, Type 2412E, with reference to the article by Professor C. W. von Sydow; also 'The Viking ale and the Rhine gold', Bo Almqvist, *Arv* 21, 1965, 115-35.

26 CROMWELL AND O'DONNELL

IFC Ms. Vol. 157: 176-83. Recorded on an Ediphone in August 1935, by Liam Mac Coisdeala, full-time collector, from Marcus Ó Neachtain, Ard Mór, Carna, County Galway.

Motifs: E501.4.1 Dogs in wild hunt; G303.3.1 The devil in human form; G303.7.1 Devil rides horse; M300-M399 Prophecies.

V FOLK PRAYERS, pages 137–139

For sources see the introductory note.

VI POPULAR CHARMS, pages 141–145

The legend which forms the background to the origin of the charm to cure a 'stitch' (pain) in the side was recorded in Irish in the 1930s. by Dr Robin Flower, from Peig Sayers on the Great Blasket Island, in West Kerry, and was transcribed from an Ediphone cylinder by Seosamh Ó Dálaigh, full-time collector, in 1947. The text is to be found in IFC. Ms. Vol. 983: 419-23.

The other charms are taken from Douglas Hyde's *Abhráin Diadha Chúige Connacht,* already mentioned.

VII PROVERBS (THREES AND FOURS), pages 147–152

The triads and other proverbs chosen for inclusion in this volume have been selected, in translation, from the following collections of Irish proverbs from Munster, Connacht and Ulster:

Seanfhocail na Muimhneach, ed. An Seabhac, 1926 (Munster);
Sean-fhocla Chonnacht, I-II, ed. Tomás Ó Máille, 1948 and 1952 (Connacht);

176 *Notes*

Seanfhocla Uladh, ed. Énrí Ó Muirgheasa, 1931 (Ulster).
All the proverbs quoted are from oral tradition. There are scores of thousands of proverbs of all kinds in the manuscripts of the Irish Folklore Department in Dublin.

VIII RIDDLES, pages 153–154

Only a very small selection of the thousands of riddles current in Ireland has been included in this volume. The Schools Collection of folklore in University College, Dublin, is a veritable 'gold mine' for researchers into this facet of Irish oral tradition.

For a selection in print, see *A Collection of Irish Riddles*, by Vernam Hull and Archer Taylor, University of California Press (Folklore Studies: 6), 1955.

IX SONGS AND BALLADS, pages 155–165

27 THE MAID OF MAGHERACLOONE
IFC Schools Ms. Vol. 929: 150-2. Received in 1939 from Ballynagearn National School, in the parish of Magheracloone, barony of Farney, County Monaghan.

28 DOWN BY MOUNT CALLAN'S SIDE
IFC Schools Ms. Vol. 609: 136-40. The song was written down in 1938 by a school-child, Mary Keane, a pupil at Kanturk National School, Connolly, Kilmaley, Co. Clare, from John Boland (52), Tulloghaboy, Connolly.

29 THE FOOT OF ROOSKA HILL
IFC Schools Ms. Vol. 487: 241-3. Received in 1939 from Ballyloghane National School, Newcastlewest, County Limerick. It was written down on 17 November 1937, by a school-child, Mary McEvoy, from her father, aged thirty-five.

Rooska Hill is in the barony of Shanid, near Newcastlewest in County Limerick.

30 FAMOUS KILDORRERY TOWN
IFC Schools Ms. Vol. 375: 156-8. The song was written down in 1938 by a school-child, Sheila Collins, aged 14, of Kildorrery, Co. Cork.

Kildorrery is a village in North Cork, near the border of County Limerick. The other towns and villages mentioned in the song are in Munster.

31 THE ALFRED DE SNOW
IFC Schools Ms. Vol. 870 : 183-6. Received from Templetown National School, in the Barony of Shelbourne, County Wexford in 1939.

A vivid account of the loss of this ship ('The Alfred de Snow') in Waterford Harbour, near Duncannon, during a storm, is given in the manuscript by the teacher, Charles Hearne, whose parents witnessed the disaster from Creadan Head, on the Waterford shore. The date of the loss of the ship is variously given as about 1875 and 1888.

Another version of the ballad is to be found, with musical notation, in *Songs of the Wexford Coast*, collected and edited by Joseph Ranson, C.C., Enniscorthy (1948), pp. 116-7.

32 FRANCIE HYNES
IFC Schools Ms. Vol. 614 : 139-42. Received from Corofin Girls' National School, Parish of Kilnaboy, Co. Clare, in 1939. The ballad was recorded in that district in January, 1938.

According to an account which accompanied the ballad, Hynes was the son of an attorney and was 'hanged in the wrong' on 11 September, 1882, for having, it was charged, murdered a man named Doolarty. As is often the case with ballads of the gallows, the earlier verses are put into the mouth of the condemned man, who proclaims his innocence, while the later ones describe the hanging.

A quite different ballad about this hanging is given in *Old Irish Street Ballads*, I, 35 (and note p. 350), Mercier Press, Cork.

Select Bibliography

The undermentioned books will give readers who do not know the Irish language an introduction to the lore of Ireland, as it is found in publications in the English tongue.

ELIZABETH ANDREWS, *Ulster Folklore*, 1913
Béaloideas (The Journal of the Folklore of Ireland Society), 1927—(in progress)
ALAN BRUFORD, *Gaelic Folktales and Mediaeval Romances*, 1969
J. J. CAMPELL, *Legends of Ireland*, 1955
LADY CHATTERTON, *Rambles in the South of Ireland*, I-II, 1839
REIDAR TH. CHRISTIANSEN, *Studies in Irish and Scandinavian Folktales*, 1959
NATHANIEL COLGAN, 'Gaelic Plant and Animal Names and associated folklore' (Clare Island Survey, *Proceedings of the Royal Irish Academy*, 1911)
PADRAIC COLUM, *The King of Ireland's Son*, 1916
   A Treasury of Irish Folklore, 1954
JEANNA COOPER-FOSTER, *Ulster Folklore*, 1951
THOMAS CROFTON CROKER, *Fairy Legends and Traditions of the South of Ireland*, 1825
   Legends of the Lakes, 1829
TOM PEETE CROSS AND CLARK HARRIS SLOVER, *Ancient Irish Tales*, 1935
JEREMIAH CURTIN, *Myths and Folklore of Ireland*, 1890
   Hero-Tales of Ireland, 1894
   Tales of the Fairies and the Ghost-World, 1895
   Irish Folk Tales, 1943 (reprint from a newspaper)
KEVIN DANAHER, *In Ireland Long Ago*, 1962
   Folktales of the Irish Countryside, 1968
DANIEL DEENY, *Peasant Lore from Gaelic Ireland*, 1901
E. ESTYN EVANS, *Irish Folkways*, 1957
ROBIN FLOWER, *The Western Island*, 1944
   The Irish Tradition, 1947
ALAN GAILEY, *Irish Folk Drama*, 1969
ALFRED PERCIVAL GRAVES, *The Irish Fairy Book*, 1938
LADY AUGUSTA GREGORY, *Poets and Dreamers*, 1903
   The Kiltartan Wonderbook, 1910
   The Kiltartan History Book, 1926
MR. AND MRS. S. C. HALL, *The South and Killarney*, 1853

Select Bibliography

JAMES HEALY, editor *Old Irish Street Ballads*, I-III 1967-1969
SAM HENRY, *Ulster Folk Tales*, 1939
VERNAM HULL and ARCHER TAYLOR, *A Collection of Irish Riddles*, 1955
B. HUNT, *Folk Tales of Breffny*, 1912
JOHN HANNON, *The King and the Cats*, 1908
DOUGLAS HYDE, *Beside the Fire*, 1890
   Legends of Saints and Sinners, 1915
JOSEPH JACOBS, *Celtic Fairy Tales*, 1892
   More Celtic Fairy Tales, 1894
P. W. JOYCE, *Old Celtic Romances*, 1961 (reprint)
MAUD JOYNT, *The Golden Legends of the Gael*, no date
PATRICK KENNEDY, *Legends of Mount Leinster*, 1855
   Legendary Fictions of the Irish Celts, 1866
   The Banks of the Boro, 1867
   The Fireside Stories of Ireland, 1870
   Evenings in the Duffrey, 1875
WILLIAM LARMINE, *West Irish Folk-Tales and Romances*, 1893
EDUMUND LEAMY, *Irish Fairy Tales*, 1906
SAMUEL LOVER, *Legends and Stories of Ireland*, 1834
BRYAN MACMAHON, *Jack O'Moora and the King of Ireland's Son*, 1950
MAIRE MAC NEILL, *The Festival of Lughnasa*, 1962
SEUMAS MAC MANUS, *In Chimney Corners*, 1899
   Donegal Fairy Stories, 1902
   Tales That Were Told, 1920
   Donegal Wonder Book, 1926
JOHN M. MARSHALL, *Popular Rhymes and Sayings of Ireland*, I-II, 1924-1926
HENRY MORRIS, *Told at the Feis*, no date
   The King of Ireland's Son, no date
PAT MULLEN, *Irish Tales*, 1938
GERARD MURPHY, *Tales from Ireland*, 1947
   Duanaire Finn, 1953
MICHAEL J. MURPHY, *At Slieve Gullion's Foot*, 1940
TOMAS O'CROHAN, *The Islandman* (translated from the Irish by Dr. Robin Flower), 1951
EILEEN O'FAOLAIN, *Irish Sagas and Folktales*, 1954
   Children of the Salmon, 1965
JOHN CANON O'HANLON ('Lageniensis'), *Irish Local Legends*, 1896
COLM O LOCHLAINN, *Irish Street Ballads*, 1939
   More Irish Street Ballads, 1965
THOMAS O'RAHILLY, *A Miscellany of Irish Proverbs*, 1922
SEAN O SUILLEABHAIN, *A Handbook of Irish Folklore*, 1942, 1963, 1971
   (and Reidar Th. Christiansen), *The Types of the Irish Folktale*, 1963
   Irish Wake Amusements, 1967
   Irish Folk Custom and Belief, 1967
   Storytelling in Irish Tradition, 1973
D. J. O'SULLIVAN, *The Bunting Collection of Irish Folk Music and Song*, I-VI, 1927-1939

SEAN O'SULLIVAN, *Folktales of Ireland*, 1966
T. G. F. PATERSON, *County Cracks*, 1939
GERTRUDE SCHOEPPERLE, *Tristan and Isolt*, I-II, 1913
JOHN MILLINGTON SYNGE, *The Aran Islands*, 1906, 1920
   In Wicklow and West Kerry, 1912
Ulster Folk Life Journal, 1955 – (in progress)
LADY WILDE, *Ancient Legends, Mystic Charms, and Superstitions of Ireland*, 1888
   Ancient Cures, Charms and Usages of Ireland, 1890
SIR WILLIAM WILDE, *Irish Popular Superstitions*, 1853
W. G. WOOD-MARTIN, *Traces of the Elder Faiths of Ireland*, I-II, 1902
W. B. YEATS, *Fairy and Folk Tales of the Irish Peasantry*, 1888
   Irish Fairy Tales, 1892

Note: Old rural buildings and craft displays may be seen at Muckross House (Killarney), Bunratty (County Limerick), Glencolmkille (County Donegal) and the Ulster Folk Museum, Cultra Manor, County Down.

Index of Tale Types

Numbers preceded by AT are from Antti Aarne and Stith Thompson, *The Types of the Folktale* 1961; those with ML are from Reidar Th. Christiansen, *The Migratory Legends* 1958.

AT 300 The Dragon Slayer	35-43
cf. AT 461 Three Hairs from the Devil's Beard	74-82, 171
cf. AT 471 The Bridge to the Other World	70-4
AT 930-949 Tales of Fate	87-90, 172
AT 931 Oedipus	67-70, 170
AT 934C* Man will Die if ever he Sees his Daughter's son	17-22, 167
AT 970 The Twining Branches	83-6, 171
AT 1137 The Ogre Blinded (Polyphemus)	22, 167
cf. AT 1149 Children Desire Ogre's Flesh	39, 168
ML 4000 'The Guntram Legend'	125-7, 174
ML 4080 The Seal Woman	116-9, 173-4
ML 5070 Midwife to the Fairies	100-104, 172-3

Motif Index

These numbers are from Stith Thompson, *Motif-Index of Folk Literature*, 1966.

B 11.10 Sacrifice of human being to dragon	35-43
B 401 Helpful horse	53-66
B 601.18 Marriage to seal	116-9
B 631.2 Human beings descended from seals	116-9
B 871.1.6 Giant cat	46-53
C 283 Tabu: eating without giving thanks	79-82
C 993 Unborn chil' affected by mother's broken tabu	90-1
D 6 Enchanted castle	43-6, 70-4, 100-4
D 327.2 Seal becomes person	116-23
D 838.8 Magic helmet	41-3
D 1004 Magic tear	22
D 1652.3.1 Cow with inexhaustible milk	17-22
D 1811.1.1 Thumb of knowledge	32
D 1840–1847 Magic invulnerability	23-9, 41-3
D 1840.3 Burning magically evaded	28-9, 37
D 1841.5 Invulnerability from weapons	29, 37-8
D 1841.6 Immunity from drowning	29, 37
D 2141 Storm produced by magic	109-12
D 2143.3 Fog produced by magic	62-4
E 102 Resuscitation by magic liquid	46-53
E 155.1 Slain warriors revive nightly	46-53
E 0–199 Resuscitation	46-53
E 489.7 Judas Iscariot appears in midst of sea on rock washed alternately by fiery and icy waves	67-70, 170
E 501.4.1 Dogs in wild hunt	135
E 631.0.1 Twining branches grow from graves of lovers	83-6, 171
E 734.1 Soul in form of butterfly	125-7, 174
E 755.3 Souls in purgatory	67-82
E 783 Vital head: retains life after being cut off	53-66
F 1 Journey to otherworld as dream of vision	70-9
F 171.1 Fat and lean kine in otherworld	78
F 234.1.6 Fairy in form of frog	100-4
F 379.2 Objects brought home from fairy land	103-4
F 420.1.2 Water-spirit as woman (water-nymph, water-nix)	116-9
F 420.1.3.3 Water-spirit as horse	113-6
F 420.5.2.1.1 Water-maiden enamours man and draws him under water	123-5
F 471.1 Nightmare	94-100
F 492 Death on horseback	113-6
F 513.0.3 Mouthless people	90-1

Motif Index 185

F 730 Extraordinary islands — 67-70, 77, 91-4
F 771.6 Phantom house: disappears at dawn — 43-6
F 989.13 Animal dives into lake and disappears — 113-6
F 1071.2.1 Enormous leap — 27-8, 31-2
G 303.3.1 The devil in human form — 75, 79, 109-12, 135
G 303.7.1 Devil rides horse — 135
G 308.1 Fight with sea/lake monster — 41-2
H 51.1 Recognition by birthmark — 69
H 900 Tasks imposed — 33-4, 50-2, 54-66, 75-9, 96-9, 105-112
H 900–1399 Tests of prowess: tasks — 33-4, 39, 50-2, 54-66, 105-12
H 1090 Tasks requiring miraculous speed — 39, 96-100
H 1141 Task: eating enormous amount — 19
H 1142 Task: drinking enormous amount — 20
H 1200ff. Quests — 40-3, 50-66, 76-82, 94-100, 105-9
H 1291 Questions asked on way to Other World — 79-82
H 1292.5 Question (on quest): How can the girl thus far avoided by suitors marry? — 82
H 1381.1 Quest for unknown parents — 54-5
J Uniting against a common enemy 18-22, 42, 48-9, 53-66, 91-3, 109-12, 130-1
J 652 Inattention to warnings — 23-30, 96-100, 105-7, 115
K 1839.12 Disguise as child in cradle — 38-9
K 1863 Death feigned to learn how soldiers are resuscitated — 49-50
K 1886.2 Mists which lead astray — 43,62
L 435.2 Self-righteous woman punished — 90-1
M 300–399 Prophecies — 19-22, 23, 30, 68, 85, 88, 111, 132-5
M 343 Parricide prophecy — 68
M 344 Mother-incest prophecy — 68
M 391.1 Fulfilment of prophecy successfully avoided — 87-90
N 511 Treasure in ground — 107-9
N 733.1 Brothers unwittingly fight against each other — 23,9
N 825.1 Childless old couple adopt hero — 54
P 556 Challenge to battle — 50-3, 55-6, 59-66
Q 221.6 Lack of trust in God punished — 90-1
Q 241 Adultery punished — 65-6
Q 286 Uncharitableness punished — 72-4, 81-2
Q 414 Punishment: burning alive — 65
Q 560.0.3 Soul of Judas tormented on rock in sea on certain days as respite from pains of hell — 70, 170
Q 560.2 Respite from hell — 70, 170
Q 566 Punishments by heat in hell — 70, 82, 170
R 10.1 Princess/maiden abducted — 74-9
R 131 Exposed or abandoned child rescued — 68
S 63 Spouse murder pact — 130-1
T 157 Fiancée forces elopement with another man — 26-7, 31
T 161 Jus primae noctis — 130, 174-5
T 551.6 Child born without mouth — 91, 172
T 575.1 Child speaks in mother's womb — 23
T 585.5 Child born with all his teeth — 39
T 640 Illegitimate children — 20, 65
V 222.1.1 Radiance fills church when saint dies — 89
V 222.7 Dead holy man stretches hand from grave to honour saint — 94
V 316 Efficacy of prayer — 82
V 510ff. Visions — 43-6, 70-82, 87-90, 91-4, 126-7, 135
Z 65.1 Red as blood, white as snow — 25

Z 72.1 A year and a day	115
Z 110 Personifications	43-6
Z 111 Death personified	43-6

General Index

Abandoned child adopted, 54
Aghadoe, 86, 171
Aill, 23–9
Alfred de Snow, 162, 177
Allegorical tale, 43–6
Almsgiving, 74, 82
Annaghdown, 114–5
Ardán, 25–9
Ard-Mhac-Léinn, 59–60
Arm severed in fight, 47
Astrology, 88
Ballyferriter, 109
Balor, 18–22, 167
Battle of Moytura, 17–18
Battle of Ventry, 35, 42
Bed throws man on to floor, 72–3
Big Man, 35–43, 168
Birthmark, 68–9
Blake, 98
Blasket Islands, 120, 125, 168, 170, 173–5
Blood, 105–9, 173
Boar hunting, 34
Bran, Finn mac Cool's dog, 40–2
Breaking of tabu, 90–1
Brian Boru, 129–31
Brother searches for sister, 74–9
Butterfly (soul), 126–7, 174
Caherlistrane, 94
Cahill, 141
Cairns, 116
Cakes of blood, 105–9, 173
Caoineadh (lament), 84–5
Card-games, 54
Castlebar, 115–6
Castles, 113–6
Céatach, 46
Chairs of gold, silver, 54
Challenges, 46, 53–66, 169
Charms, 94, 141–5, 175
Children of Lir, 23
Children of Tuireann, 23
Clare, 98

Claregalway, 95–100
Clontarf, 129
Cloonakilleen, 98
Coffin floats on sea, 93
Conán Maol, 47
Conchobhar, king of Ulster, 23–9
Conneelys, 116–9, 173
Contests, 33–4, 39, 50–2, 54–66, 105–12
Cormac mac Airt, 30–2
Coumeenole, 120, 174
Creeveen de Búrc, 113–6, 173
Cregg, 98
Cromwell, 132–5, 175
Cú, the Smith's Son, 53–66
'Danes', 129–32, 174–5
'Danish beer', 130–1, 175
Death, 46, 169
de Barra, Seoirse, 113–6, 173
de Búrc, Creeveen, 113–6, 173
Deirdre, 23–9, 167
Derryveagh, 93–4
Devil, 74–9, 86, 105, 109–12, 135, 173, 175
Diarmaid O Duibhne, 30–4, 167–8
Didactic tale, 79
Dingle, 109–12
Dolmens, 30, 168
Donegal, 18, 91, 117
Doolarty, 164
Doolough, 157–8, 177
Down, 93
Downpatrick, 93–4
Dreams and nightmares, 94–100, 172
Drinking test, 20
Drop falls incessantly, 81–2
Dunquin, 120–2
Eagle takes man on back, 99
Eating test, 19–20
Elopement, 23–34
Enchanted rocks, 93
Errismore, 117
Exempla tales, 79, 90

General Index

Fairies, 100–4
Farmer's life best, 70–4
Fat and lean kine, 78
Fate, 87–90, 171–2
Ffrench, 98
Fianna, 30–46, 168–9
Finn mac Cool, 30–46, 168–9
Flaherty, 116
Flood every seven years, 99
Folk medicine, 141–5
Forge, 134
Foxes, 97–8
Frog (fairy woman), 100–4, 172–3
Gaibhde the Smith, 18–22, 167
Galway, 94–100, 114
Gartan, 91
Geasa (magical injunctions) 20, 36, 54–66, 122, 169
Ghosts, 81, 105–9
Giants, 18–22, 35–43, 55–6, 60–1
Glas Ghaibhleann, 18–22
Glendowan, 79
Glenveagh, 22
Golden chair, 54
Grace after Meals, 82
Gráinne, 30–4, 167–8
Gráinne Bharóid, 38–9
Great Cat of the Cave, 51–3
Greece, 55–66
Guntram legend, 125–7, 174
Gweedore, 91
Hags, 61–6
Hand, The, 157
Hill of the Saints, 91
Horse helps hero, 56–66
Hunger unsatisfied, 80–82
Hynes, Francie, 163–5, 177
Illaunbwee, 124
Iveragh, 123–5
Judas Iscariot, 67–70, 170
Jus Primae Noctis, 21–2, 130–1
Kennedy, Dermot, 95–100
Keogh, 141
Kildorrery, 160–1, 176–7
King Edward, 161
King of the Bridge, 50–3
King of the Churchyard, 50–3
King of Greece, 55–66
King of Ireland, 24–9, 53–66
King of Leinster, 96–100
King of Scotland, 27, 96–100
King of the Sea, 118
King of Spain, 135
King of Sunday, 74–9, 170–1
Kinsale, 158

Knockatoo, 116
Knockma, 95
Lake monster, 36, 41–2
Land of the Big Men, 35–43
Leacht Seoirse (Lough George), 113–6, 173
Lettercath, 131
Loughafoor, 115
Lough Swilly, 93
Lough Veagh, 22
Lugh, 17, 168
Mac Amhlaoimh, 132–5
Mac Codrum, 117
Mac Mhaol, 60–1
Magheracloone, 156–7, 176
Magheraroarty, 18
Magical enchantment, 43–6, 62, 91–3
Magical powers, 22, 49, 105–12
Magical protection, 29, 35–43
Magic castle, 43–6, 72–73, 124, 126
Magic food, 45, 72, 105–9
Magic swords, 56
Man (as baby) in cradle, 38–39, 168
Manannán, 23–4
Maol, 21
March cock, 105–9
Mare becomes woman, 66
Mary Magdalen, 69
Mass (vision) 74–9
May Day, 117–8
Mélusine, 113
Monasteries, 97, 133
Mount Callan, 157–8, 176
Mullogue, 21
Mystical garden, 72, 78
Mystical glen, 43, 72
Mystical house, 43, 72
Mystical island, 70, 77
Naoise, 25–9
Nix, 113–6
O'Connor of Sligo, 97–9
O'Donnell, 132–5
Oedipus, 67
O Fáilbhe, Cluasach, 113
O'Friels, 92–3
Oisín, 43–4
Oscar, 43–4
O'Shea, 116
Otherworld journey, 43–6, 70–79, 99–104
Perseus story, 35
Personifications, 43–6, 169
Poisonous eye-tear, 22
Polyphemus, 18
Poor scholar, 88–90, 108–9

General Index 189

Prayers (traditional) 137–9
Priests, 70–4
Prophecies, 88, 175–6
Proverbs, 147–52
Punishments, 65, 67–74, 79–82, 87–9, 105–9, 113–6, 120–3, 130–1, 135
Quests, 40–3, 50–66, 76–82, 94–100, 105–9, 169
Rat follows man, 114
Red Fox of Kesh, 97–100
Resuscitation, 48–50, 105–9
Rewards, 70–4, 82, 107–12, 120–3, 134
Riddles, 153–4, 176
Ring enforces truth, 65
Roof of lead, 28–9
Rooska Hill, 159–60, 176
'Runs' (rhetorics) in tales, 29, 46–66, 119, 169
Sailor, 109–12, 173
Saint Brendan, 67
Saint Brigid, 139
Saint Colmcille (Columba), 91–4, 139, 172
Saint Joseph, 74–9
Saint Patrick, 71, 94, 145, 161
Saviour, 69, 74–9, 137–45, 164
Schoolmaster, 70–4
Scotland, 23–9, 30, 33, 117, 130, 137
Seals, 116–23, 173–4
Sea-woman, 116–9, 123–5
Seoirse de Barra, 113–6, 173
Severed arm strikes man, 48
Shell-fish as food, 35–6
Sign of the Cross, 92
Silver road, 58
Skelligs Rocks, 111–2

Slammon, Sean, 94–100
Sligo, 34, 97–8
Slua Sí (fairy host) 100
Songs and ballads, 155–65, 176–7
Sons of Gor, 93
Sons of Uisneach, 23–9, 30, 167
Soul as butterfly, 126–7, 174
Sow and her Litter, 50–3
Spirit, 109–12, 113–6, 173
Stepmother, 53–66
Stone cairn, 116
Submarine court, 123–5, 174
Tasks and tests, 33–4, 39, 50–66, 75–9, 96–9, 105–12
Teeth of king missing, 59–66, 169
Threshing in Heaven, 99–100
Thumb of Knowledge, 32
Tón an Chroic, 97–8
Tory Island, 18–22, 91–4, 172
Treachery, 130–1
Treasure, 105–9
Tristan and Iseult, 23, 167–8
Tuatha Dé Danann, 18
Turloughmore, 95–100
Ulster Cycle of Storytelling, 23, 30, 167
Uncharitableness punished, 74, 79–82
Urlar, 97–100
Virgin Mary, 137–45, 165
Warriors fight, 28–9, 46–66
Water-horses, 113–6, 173
Weapon against wave, 123–5
Weasel, 114
Woman (alive) in coffin, 46–7
Women's crooked aim, 20, 167
Wooing of Etaín, 17